SELF-CONFIDENCE
STRATEGIES FOR WOMEN

SELF-CONFIDENCE
Strategies for Women

Essential Tools to Increase Self-Esteem and Achieve Your True Potential

Leslie Theriot Herhold, MSW, LCSW, PMH-C

Illustrated by Niki Fisher

ROCKRIDGE
PRESS

Interior and Cover Designer: Erin Yeung
Art Producer: Sue Bischofberger
Editor: Shabnam Sigman and Marisa A. Hines
Production Manager: Michael Kay
Production Editor: Melissa Edeburn
Illustration © 2020 Niki Fisher
Author photo courtesy of Carlie Anne Collective, 2019

ISBN: Print 978-1-64739-146-1 | eBook 978-1-64739-147-8

R0

This book is dedicated to my amazing daughter, Elizabeth, who loves books as much as I do, and thinks I am so cool for writing one. May you always have the self-confidence to be exactly who you are: strong, smart, and beautiful inside and out. I love you all the time.

Contents

Introduction

Like many of you, I struggled with low self-confidence and poor self-esteem as a young girl and into my early 20s. It makes me terribly sad to look back and see how desperately I tried to fit in and how little confidence I had in myself, but I now realize those early struggles were shaping me into the woman, therapist, and mother I would one day become. For that, I am grateful.

As a psychotherapist who focuses exclusively on women's mental health, the topic of self-confidence comes up just as frequently as the symptoms that lead my clients to call for an appointment. The majority of my work is counseling women who are struggling with motherhood, infertility, pregnancy loss, and other life transitions, but self-confidence issues are often present. The relationship we have with ourselves affects how we interact with others, care for our children, and choose our partners. I see this dynamic every day in the women I work with.

The great thing about being a woman treating other women is being able to say *I understand*, and my clients know I do. Even when our experiences differ, they know that I know what it means to be a woman in modern society. I never recommend a strategy or a self-care technique that I don't use in my own life.

I have gleaned everything in this book from my experiences as a woman—a wife, mother, and daughter—as well as from my nearly 15 years as a clinical social worker. I have used every strategy with the women in my practice.

This book is not a substitute for therapy with a compassionate and competent clinician, however, and it should not be used as stand-alone treatment for symptoms that are causing significant distress or depression. If you are experiencing symptoms that are disrupting your life or your ability to maintain functioning, please contact your physician or see this book's Resources (page 115) for information on choosing a therapist who can help.

Throughout the book, I refer specifically to "women" and "gender," "husband" and "partner." Please know I am coming from a place of inclusion, and I am speaking to all women who identify as such, regardless of sexual orientation. All identifying information and details in the examples have been changed. None of the scenarios reflects that of a single client.

When writing this book, I wanted to focus on coping strategies for, rather than causes of, low self-confidence. This is not to say the *whys* are not important, because they are. But when you make the decision to purchase a book like this, you are looking for concrete solutions right now. This book will give you the tools to facilitate the necessary changes in your thinking and belief patterns that will lead you to higher levels of self-confidence and overall happiness.

I encourage you to read through the chapters in order because they build on previous chapters. The tools and coping skills are linked together in a specific way to increase your confidence as you move forward. I also highly recommend keeping a journal to keep you focused and to record your progress.

I am so excited to share this information, and I sincerely believe it will bring about amazing and noticeable changes in your life. I hope you reach an entirely new level of love and appreciation for yourself.

Please keep me posted and let me know if this book was helpful on your journey to confidence.

I cannot wait to hear from you.

Take care,

Leslie

PART I
The Foundation

Part 1 of this book discusses basic concepts related to self-confidence and the theoretical framework behind the strategies outlined in this book. Depending on your professional background and your previous experience, some of this information may seem pretty basic, and some may come as a surprise. Either way, I encourage you to hang on, because these concepts serve as the foundation for the rest of the book. Part 2 is where we really explore the strategies and dive into the good stuff. Before you know it, you'll have all the tools you need to begin feeling better about yourself.

You have made the important decision to boost your self-confidence. It's not an easy process, but I have no doubt you can do it. I've seen so many women change their beliefs about themselves using these methods. It's an incredible process to witness, and I am so excited to give you the tools you need to make these changes within yourself.

Before we get started, I need you to do three things:

1. Grab a cup of coffee (or tea, water—whatever you prefer).

2. Get your notebook and a pen or a highlighter.

3. Say "I've got this." Yes, out loud. Seriously.

Now take a deep breath, and let's begin.

CHAPTER 1

Understanding Self-Confidence

Renee, 36, is a stay-at-home mother of two young daughters. Prior to having children, she was a full-time dental hygienist. She struggles with this transition, often feeling guilty for not contributing to the family financially. She is filled with shame because she misses her full-time job, her pre-pregnancy body, and using her brain for something more than mothering. She exercises daily, restricts what she eats, and constantly compares herself to women she follows on social media.

Renee's mother was extremely self-critical. She was always on a diet and critiquing her own weight, hair, and physical features. Renee's mother also turned that criticism toward Renee and other women. Renee frequently heard things like, "Did you see what she was wearing? She looked like a marshmallow," "Gosh, Aunt Sally has really put on some weight," "Are you sure that's what you want to wear?" "Do you really need a second helping?" Over and over Renee received the message that her physical appearance was important. She learned others would judge her by her appearance. She believed her self-worth was tied to her weight.

Renee now suffers from symptoms of anxiety and low self-esteem. She often feels overwhelmed, indecisive, and discontent. Her need to control and her lack of self-confidence leads to conflict in her marriage. She frequently overreacts and becomes easily frustrated with her children. She often finds herself gossiping about other women, which leads to more feelings of shame. She isn't sure if she truly likes the women she calls friends. She is constantly scrolling through social media sites and comparing herself to other women. She shops online, spending a great deal of money on hair products, clothing, and makeup. She has gotten into the habit of drinking wine in the evenings as a way to relax and unwind.

One day, while in an intense power struggle with her 4-year-old over her choice of outfit for school pictures, Renee had a flashback to her own childhood, when these power struggles were frequent. She looked at her confident, spirited daughter, who was wearing her favorite PAW Patrol T-shirt and flowered tights, and decided she did not want to pass on her self-confidence struggles to her daughters. This was a pivotal moment that changed not only Renee's own life, but also the self-esteem of her young children.

Later we will revisit Renee and discuss how she was able to use the strategies in this book to implement important changes.

What Is Self-Confidence?

In my work as a clinical therapist, the topic of self-confidence comes up frequently. So many women find themselves lacking in confidence, unable to recognize how they got to this place. Renee's story is just one example of how self-confidence struggles can manifest in a woman's life, affecting her relationships, self-esteem, and overall happiness. It may sound familiar to you, even if you have very different circumstances. This is because although your self-confidence is unique, the ways in which it affects your life are very similar to those of other women.

What do you think of when you hear the term *self-confident*? Do you associate self-confidence with concepts such as *self-assurance*, *self-esteem*, or *self-worth*? Or do you associate being self-confident with less positive characteristics, such as *overbearing*, *arrogant*, and *pretentious*?

Several factors can influence the way you view self-confidence, including your upbringing and how others perceive it. Your previous experiences also shape your viewpoint, and so does whether you were allowed to express confidence and assurance in a way that others accepted.

So what exactly is self-confidence, and how do we get it?

According to *Merriam-Webster*, it's "confidence in oneself and in one's powers and abilities." To expand on this definition, let's also add that being self-confident is intrinsically related to self-esteem. If you have positive feelings about your abilities you probably have positive feelings about yourself, and vice versa. Likewise, if you do not have positive feelings about your abilities, you are less likely to have positive feelings about yourself.

Where Does Self-Confidence Originate?

As mentioned, self-confidence may be tied to messages you received as a young girl about yourself, your abilities, and your appearance as well as societal norms.

If you were told, for example, "girls do not play rough," "girls are not as strong as boys," "people will like you more if you're pretty/thin/popular," you might have processed these statements as absolute truths. If you wanted to play sports with the boys but were not allowed to, you learned the message "you are not strong enough" or "it does not matter what you want." Both of these messages are damaging, and if not corrected can lead to decreased confidence.

These messages can be extremely subtle rather than explicitly stated. It's your *perception* of these messages that registered in your subconscious and is most likely to influence you later in life. As a child, you processed these messages through a very different lens of understanding and emotional maturity. We will challenge these messages, or self-beliefs, later in the book.

Let's look at another example of how messages learned in childhood can influence self-esteem and self-confidence.

If you were frequently complimented on your appearance and physical features at the expense of other characteristics such as intelligence, strength, and kindness, you may have believed that people, even your parents, liked you because of these traits. Remember, these messages are filtered through a child's understanding of the world, rather than an adult's ability to rationally consider what is being said. Therefore, you may have perceived the message as "I will be loved as long as I am beautiful and well-dressed." The damaging aspect of this thought is that self-confidence that relies on external sources is not true or lasting. When confidence is tied to others' perceptions, as in beauty and popularity, it is a very fragile concept that can be annihilated by the opinion of one person, one bad hair day, or five additional pounds.

As a young girl, you may have modeled your beliefs about self-confidence after those of the important women in your life. If you were lucky enough to be surrounded by confident, self-assured female role models, chances are you absorbed positive beliefs about self-confidence by observing these women. If, however, you were surrounded by women like Renee's mother, you would be more likely to absorb negative beliefs about self-confidence that could affect you for the rest of your life.

If you were told you were smart, capable, and strong, and that you could be whoever and whatever you wanted when you grew up, those statements became part of your healthy inner monologue. If you were told you were stupid, if you felt like you were a disappointment to the people you loved, if your weight and eating habits were constantly questioned and analyzed, a decrease in self-confidence would be expected.

You may be saying, "Oh, great. I had terrible role models for confidence as a child. So then it's hopeless?"

Absolutely not. If you were fortunate enough to have people in your life who nurtured your self-confidence, then you have a receptive foundation on which to build greater levels of confidence. If you did not have this reinforcement, first and foremost you can take steps to establish a healthy foundation. It is never too late to change your story. You are brave to begin this journey and to recognize the need to love yourself fully. But in order to make real changes in your self-confidence, you have to recognize the origins of your issues. Healing from these experiences takes courage, but the fact that you are reading this proves you have the desire to change.

Imagine self-confidence as a skyscraper. Although the foundations of self-confidence are built in childhood, multiple layers, like stories of a building, are added over time through your experiences and interactions with the outside world. You receive messages through your interactions with teachers, peers, coaches, co-workers, and even strangers. You receive messages from family and friends. You receive messages through social media (more on this later). Your experiences also shape your self-confidence, either negatively or positively. When you are faced with difficult situations, your level of confidence in your ability to persevere plays a huge role in how you approach your circumstances, and your perception of how well you handled a situation either reinforces or contradicts your beliefs about yourself.

What Self-Confidence Is Not

Self-confidence is not arrogance or narcissism. Being self-confident does not mean you put down others in order to make yourself feel better, and it does not mean you believe you are better than others. It also does not mean you're a bitch or you're difficult to deal with. It comes from a place of acceptance of yourself *exactly as you are*, regardless of other people's opinions and actions. This doesn't mean that self-confident women ignore the feelings of others. Rather, self-confident women do not feel bad about themselves when they have negative interactions with others. They do not allow others to make them feel worse about themselves, because they are confident in their abilities and their worth.

> ### THOUGHT EXERCISE:
> ### Self-Confident Women
>
> Think of the most self-confident woman you know. What do you admire about her? How does she embody the concept of self-confidence?

Reasons for Low Self-Confidence

The following sections focus on common contributors to low self-confidence. Even with the presence of one or more of these factors, you are not doomed to a life of low self-confidence. Although these scenarios may exist through no fault of your own, you do have the option of identifying the ways in which you have control over them. We begin by placing our focus on some of the general factors that can negatively affect self-confidence for both men and women. Later, we dive deeper into a discussion about factors unique to women.

Anxiety and Depression

The term *anxiety disorders* encompasses a fairly broad spectrum. Some of the more well-known conditions include Generalized Anxiety Disorder, Post-Traumatic Stress Disorder, Specific Phobia, Social Anxiety Disorder, Agoraphobia, Separation Anxiety Disorder, Panic Disorder, and Obsessive-Compulsive Disorder. In general, anxiety symptoms can include panic, severe worry, need to control, obsessive thinking, and physiological responses such as increased heart rate and agitation. Anxiety can also manifest through irritability, frustration, and anger. Anxiety is the most common presenting problem I see in my clinical practice with women.

The term *mood disorders* encompasses Major Depressive Disorder and both Bipolar I and II Disorders. Mood disorders are characterized by disturbances in one's mood, whether very low (as in depression) or with highs and lows associated with the bipolar disorders. Mild symptoms of depression can manifest during various life transitions and events, and as long as they do not linger or affect functioning, the patient generally improves by using good coping skills. Serious symptoms of depression are more pervasive, and they affect overall outlook, functioning, mood, and relationships. These symptoms usually last for at least two weeks, and consist of a persistently depressed mood, lack of interest, marked changes in appetite and sleep, and difficulty coping with daily life activities and responsibilities. Depression also hurts physically, and patients often report accompanying aches and pains.

Most of the preceding information was considered taboo for many years because of the stigma surrounding mental health, but this trend is slowly fading in the United States. This is good, because the lifetime rates of anxiety and mood disorders for adults in the U.S. are 31.1 percent and 21.4 percent, respectively, according to the National Institutes of Mental Health in 2017. And the rates for women are higher in both categories, which has a huge impact on children and families.

Even though there is ample evidence that anxiety and depression are the result of a combination of brain chemistry, genetics, and stressful events, the shame attached to a mental health diagnosis can lead to decreased self-esteem and self-confidence. At worst, untreated anxiety and depression can be extremely dangerous, and at best they interfere deeply with the ability to function within the world. If you are experiencing any symptoms that worry you, please seek out help and support.

See Resources (page 115) for starting points for getting the help you need.

Life Circumstances, Difficult Situations, or Hardships

Your perception of how well you handle adversity plays a role in how confident you are in yourself and your abilities. The way you approach adversity is influenced by how confident you are in your capacity to handle difficult events. For example, if you lose your job but you have been unemployed before and handled it well, you would be more inclined to tell yourself, "I will find another job, an even better one. But until this happens, I will take some side jobs to make ends meet. Everything will be fine." This sounds like someone who is confident that she is hirable and that she can do whatever it takes to stay afloat.

Taking this one step further, let's say you land your dream job, but then your hot-water heater floods your house. Because you already know you can handle difficult situations, you would likely approach this scenario with confidence in yourself (along with some aggravation and possibly tears, but that's perfectly reasonable). Once the situation is resolved, your self-confidence is once again strengthened by your ability to handle the mess without breaking down.

Now imagine that when you lost your job, your first thoughts were, "I'm such a loser. No wonder I was let go again. How am I going to get through this?" These words don't instill much confidence in yourself or your abilities to persevere. If your hot-water heater flooded, too, you probably wouldn't handle it very well. This could cause a domino effect, with every negative event reinforcing your lack of confidence in yourself.

Another factor that impacts self-confidence is your exposure to healthy coping skills in childhood. How did the adults in your life respond to stressful or difficult circumstances? Did they blame others and play the victim, or did they roll up their sleeves and remain positive? When you fell off your bike, failed a test, or missed the winning soccer goal, were you encouraged to get back up, dust off your pants, and try again? Were you told that mistakes are okay and do not define you as a person? The way you were treated in these situations helped shape your self-confidence, cultivate your ability to handle failure, and determine whether you have any tendencies toward perfectionism.

Society and Media

Mainstream news, the internet, social media, the entertainment industry, books, and magazines reflect an ideal of what it means to be male and female in modern society. These norms have shifted over time, but one thing has remained constant: the influence of media on what people buy, how they dress, and the way they view the world. Commercials can give you a sudden desire for pizza, Pinterest can make you want to rearrange your living room, and stories in the news can lead you to believe the world is a dangerous and scary place. It can be difficult to filter out what is not helpful, as we process many of these messages subconsciously. You may only recognize the effect after the fact, such as when you are eating the pizza, shifting the furniture, and buying a particular brand of shampoo.

So how does this affect self-confidence?

How do you feel after watching a tragic news story, a celebrity reality show, or a romantic comedy? You may experience feelings of impotence, fear, shame, or even jealousy. You may process these images as absolute truths about the way the world and relationships are supposed to be. You are constantly receiving messages from the people in your community and social media. These messages, whether positive or negative, are reflected in your view of yourself and the world around you. The next section discusses social media specifically and its influence on women's self-esteem.

Factors Unique to Women

In my clinical practice I have identified a few factors that are most likely to negatively impact women. The following sections delve into these conditions, behaviors, and events from a woman's perspective. Although we do not have power over all the circumstances of our lives, we can control how we respond to our situations.

Brain Chemistry

Because of the complex relationship between hormones and brain chemistry, women are at a higher risk of mood changes during certain hormonal transitions, such as puberty, the perinatal period (pregnancy and postpartum), the premenstrual period (i.e., PMS), and perimenopause. Fluctuating hormones can influence body image, mood, and energy levels. Women report changes in their libido, moods, sleep habits, energy levels, appetites, and overall feelings of well-being. Most therapists will (and should) encourage new clients to discuss these symptoms with a health care provider so routine bloodwork can rule out hormonal imbalances. It can be helpful to keep a record of your energy levels, moods, and sleep quality in relation to your menstrual cycle, and look for patterns you can share with your health care provider.

Gender Roles in Society

Society tends to emphasize women who are mothers, and views women who don't want, or cannot have, children as "other." There is also an ideal of femininity continually portrayed in magazines, movies, and social media that holds women to impossible standards of beauty and body shape. This is slowly changing, but we can still do more to ensure young girls have well-rounded role models for what it means to be a woman.

There's no doubt that traditional gender stereotypes can be damaging. Many parents now encourage their sons to express emotions and to play dress-up, and urge their daughters to play in the mud, protect themselves, and keep their bodies strong and healthy. Unfortunately, this was likely not your childhood experience.

Having an appearance, a career, or a family life that diverges from female societal norms can diminish self-confidence if you have internalized these norms. If, on the other hand, you have internalized these norms as ridiculous or antiquated, your self-confidence would not be affected.

Society still upholds and rewards the typical gender role of the confident, successful, and strong male, but a confident, successful, and strong *female* can be perplexing. Sometimes these women are labeled *overbearing*, *arrogant*, *bitch*, or *ball-buster*, to name just a few. We are still deeply affected by society's definition of what it means to be a woman.

Career

Many women experience negative interactions with others in the years prior to beginning a career. Post-secondary education is a time of great growth for many women, with the possibility of increased confidence and autonomy. This can also be a time of further exposure to societal norms and romantic relationships, which can reinforce or decrease self-confidence. Learning experiences during this time are not limited to the classroom.

These experiences continue with the development of a career. Job searching, interviewing, and adjusting to new expectations while managing a family or social life can place tremendous pressure on women. We are bombarded by the idea of "having it all" (i.e., being superwoman), which can be encouraging (because, yes, women can do anything) but can also lead to feelings of failure when we are held to impossible standards and unrealistic expectations.

The workplace can be a landmine of confidence busters, including being excluded from a social event, being passed up for a promotion, or making an error. Don't even get me started on the many other offenses women can face, such as pay disparity, pumping breast milk in a closet (or, worse, a restroom), sexual harassment, impossible expectations of the work–life balance, and so on.

Parenthood

Society categorically divides women into mothers and non-mothers. The choice of whether to start a family is deeply complex and personal. Many women will report that their self-confidence is affected by this status, especially if things do not go the way they planned—for example, if a woman struggles with fertility, or becomes a mother much earlier than expected. A woman can gain confidence in her status as mother, but she can also lose confidence if she does not want to have children, or she is among the one in eight women in America who deals with infertility.

In my clinical work with women struggling with fertility challenges, this decrease in confidence is often addressed in therapy because it has the potential to negatively impact her self-esteem and her relationships. Women who have difficulty conceiving or carrying pregnancies to term often report feelings of frustration and anger toward their bodies. They feel defective or less of a woman because they believe they have failed to achieve a basic biological function.

On the flip side, women who experience significant struggles with transitioning to motherhood (like Renee at the beginning of the chapter) report devastating blows to their self-confidence. When life does not match their expectations, it can lead to disappointment, shame, and decreased self-esteem.

Social Media and Self-Image

Self-image is the way you see yourself in the world, and how you believe the world sees you. Decreased levels of self-confidence and self-esteem lead to a negative self-image. If you look in the mirror and don't like what you see, if you are not happy in your own skin, and if you are unhappy with yourself, your situation, or your circumstances, you are more likely to project that unhappiness onto others. Other people may in turn respond to you in a negative way, which will then reinforce the negative self-image. This is why you are more likely to believe that others see you negatively if you have a poor self-image. It becomes a negative feedback loop that must be interrupted before it can be reversed.

Social media can also influence self-image. Seeing yourself reflected in positive role models who have a similar ethnic background and body type can boost your self-image. This is why it is so important for magazines, television, and movies to represent a wide variety of girls and women.

Social media updates us on what's going on in the world, keeps us connected with family and friends in other parts of the country, provides us with entertainment, and helps our businesses grow, but it also has some drawbacks.

Many women now turn to social media for advice, support, connection, and distraction. Spending too much time on social media can increase anxiety because of the sheer volume of information and opinions. Even though we know social media illustrates only a curated snapshot of an individual's life, it is human nature to compare. When women compare themselves to other women, this can lead to a decrease in self-confidence and an increase in self-doubt. Likewise, following

Instagram celebrities and influencers can also lead to the comparison trap and reinforce feelings of being less-than.

When women use social media to distract themselves from and avoid the real world, it generally leads to perpetuating the feelings they were seeking to avoid in the first place—self-doubt, shame, and guilt.

Relationships

Are you familiar with the saying "If you walk like a duck, quack like a duck, and hang out with other ducks, people will think you're a duck?" I heard this repeatedly in childhood, and I never forgot it. Basically, it's a warning to be very careful about choosing your friends because people will make assumptions about you based on who you associate with. Not only that, but you will also begin to make assumptions about *yourself* based on the people in your social group.

If you surround yourself with negative people, you will become increasingly negative. If you associate with women who backstab, gossip, and compare, your self-confidence will be adversely affected. It is difficult to be around someone who is always complaining because she may not welcome or appreciate any positivity from you. Good friends make you feel better about yourself, celebrate your successes, and encourage you to be the best version of yourself. Bad friends can damage your self-esteem and lead to a poor self-image.

It's not only friendships that can lead to a decrease in self-confidence; any unhealthy relationship with poor boundaries or a lack of respect—whether it's a friend, parent, sibling, or romantic partner—can negatively impact the way you feel about yourself.

According to the National Coalition Against Domestic Violence, one in three women has experienced some form of physical violence by an intimate partner, and 48.4 percent of women have experienced at least one episode of psychological aggression (abuse via control, isolation, humiliation, or stalking). These numbers are both staggering and heartbreaking. Intimate partner violence has devastating physical as well as psychological impacts, and the long-term effects can be extremely damaging.

A relationship does not have to include this level of aggression or violence to negatively affect your self-esteem and self-confidence. Any romantic relationship in which you feel you are not allowed to be yourself, wear what you want to wear, or maintain contact with friends and family is considered controlling. If you feel that your partner does not value your wants and needs or respect your sexual boundaries, or if you suspect your partner has been unfaithful, your self-confidence will decrease.

The Dangers of Self-Medication

According to the National Institute on Alcohol Abuse and Alcoholism, alcohol consumption among women in the United States is increasing. Many women, like Renee earlier in the chapter, drink to self-medicate symptoms of anxiety and depression, which is incredibly dangerous. Alcohol is a depressant, and problem drinking often leads to worsening symptoms of anxiety and depression, plus shame and guilt if the use is hidden from family and friends. Over time the consequences of problem drinking can include decreased self-confidence, health problems, relationship strain, and legal issues. If you suspect you have been using alcohol or other substances as a Band-Aid, consult the Resources (page 115) for help.

THOUGHT EXERCISE:
Influences

Can you recall any specific experiences in your life that may have negatively influenced your self-confidence? What about experiences that positively influenced your self-confidence?

The Benefits of Improved Self-Confidence

Why is self-confidence so important? There are too many benefits to include in this chapter, but here are a few big ones.

More Resilience

There is no doubt that terrible, unfair things happen. As discussed earlier, your self-confidence informs how you respond to stressful and difficult situations. It's amazing not only to survive hardships, but also come out on the other side with a deeper understanding of yourself. Having faith in yourself and in your ability to grow and learn from your mistakes is a benefit of a healthy self-confidence. Thriving despite injustices and disappointments, because you know your self-worth, is another way self-confidence will benefit your life.

Improved Relationships

A positive self-confidence will influence those around you. When you feel good about yourself, you're more likely to see the good in others. When you are confident in your own skin, you are able to admit your mistakes and shortcomings and know they do not define you. You take personal responsibility for your role in arguments or miscommunications rather than passing the blame. Modeling positive self-confidence also encourages others to become the best version of themselves.

Increased Motivation

When you believe you are capable of doing great things and you are confident in your ability to persevere and move forward even when facing difficulties, you are more likely to seek out opportunities that will improve your life. You are more excited about trying new things. You open yourself up to all the possibilities life has in store for you. When you are self-confident, you move forward even when it is scary and the outcome is unknown.

STRATEGIES

Take a moment to implement the following strategies for getting into a positive mindset.

- Find a quote about self-confidence that resonates with you and makes you feel better. Write it on a sticky note and place it on your bathroom mirror, your steering wheel, your laptop, and anywhere else you'd like. If you can't choose just one quote, use more. My favorites include, "You got this!"(courtesy of my five-year-old), "You're in the arena!" (from Brené Brown's *Daring Greatly*), and, for any Jen Sincero fans out there, "You are a badass!"

- Identify your primary support person—someone who loves you unconditionally, is there for you at your worst, and cheers for you at your best. This could be a friend, partner, sibling, or parent. Identify this person and tell him or her you're reading this book. Some of the exercises can be uncomfortable, so make sure you have someone you trust (besides me) to be your supporter and cheerleader.

- This one is extremely important. TAKE A BREAK FROM SOCIAL MEDIA. Ideally, stay away from it the whole time you're reading this book and working through the chapters. At the very least, take a couple of days off and pay careful attention to how you feel. This includes Facebook, Instagram, and Snapchat. (I may be missing some, but you get the drift.)

Putting Strategies into Practice

Let's revisit Renee and see how she implemented these strategies.

Renee's improvement begins with the *decision* to interrupt her cycle of negative self-confidence, her *courage* to begin the very uncomfortable work of identifying the roots of her self-esteem struggles, and her *motivation* to challenge everything she has believed about herself.

Once Renee makes this decision, there's no stopping her. She buys a journal, throws out the wine, and temporarily deactivates her social media accounts. Because her husband is her primary emotional support, she gets him on board with her plan. While dropping off her daughter at school, she avoids the gossip and invites another frazzled mom and her baby to coffee. The next time Renee speaks with her mother on the phone, she uses firm but kind boundaries to limit her exposure to any negativity.

Then she gets to work using the tools outlined in this book. She gets clear about her goals, acknowledges her less helpful characteristics, and identifies her negative thought patterns. When she hits roadblocks or becomes discouraged, she thinks of her daughter in the PAW Patrol shirt with the unbearably brokenhearted expression on her sweet face. She thinks of herself as a little girl, imagines hugging her and telling her she is smart, strong, and brave. This is where she finds her motivation. Slowly but surely, she begins to notice a change in herself. This increases her confidence and overall happiness. She begins to thrive, and her family thrives along with her.

Let's get you started on the path of self-love and self-confidence. It is possible for every woman. Time to get your tool kit ready.

CHAPTER 2

Assembling Your Tool Kit and Setting Goals

Ashley has a passion for reading, especially fantasy novels. The librarians at her college know her by name and frequently set aside new titles for her. When Ashley was in high school, she dreamed of becoming an author of children's books. She had visions of herself as the next J. K. Rowling or Tui Sutherland. Ashley's parents enjoyed hearing her stories, but they did not encourage her desire to become a writer. They told her that being an author was not a "real career," and that she would not be able to make a living by writing. Ashley believed them. She decided her dreams were not realistic, and that she needed to make smarter choices for her future.

Ashley enrolls in college with a major in accounting. She begins work as a part-time runner for her uncle's accounting firm, with the expectation that she will eventually join as a CPA. Mathematical concepts have always come easily to Ashley, and even though she finds accounting boring, she continues with these plans so she will not disappoint her parents.

When Ashley takes a creative writing class in her senior year, she realizes how much she misses writing. Her professor notices Ashley's talent and encourages her to join the Creative Writing Club. Ashley declines, blaming her part-time job. As much as she loves writing, she believes this would be a waste of time.

Ashley goes on to graduate and begins working full-time for her uncle. Now 26 years old, she is well on her way to a successful career as an accountant. The fact that she is bored and unfulfilled is secondary to the fact that her parents are very proud. But Ashley grows tired and becomes burned out. She begins to show symptoms of anxiety and depression. Her social life is nonexistent, and she hasn't been on a date in months. She is terribly unhappy but feels trapped and unable to identify the source of her discontent.

While cleaning out her closet, Ashley finds a box of papers from college, including all her assignments from the creative writing class. She sits on the floor, reading her stories, and cries. She realizes she needs to change her career, but she feels completely powerless to do anything about it.

Using Principles of CBT and ACT

The following sections provide an overview of the theoretical framework behind two popular therapeutic approaches: Cognitive Behavioral Therapy and Acceptance and Commitment Therapy. Both models can increase self-confidence in significant ways, and they are incorporated into the strategies you will learn in part 2.

CBT, ACT, and Exposure Therapy

Cognitive Behavioral Therapy (CBT) is based on the belief that your thoughts influence your feelings and emotions, which then cause a particular mood. This mood leads to behavior that reinforces your thoughts and emotions in a continuous cycle. Changing your mindset and actively addressing negative thoughts will improve your self-confidence. Many people enjoy CBT work because it enables you to maintain a sense of control and power over your reactions and feelings. CBT is discussed in further detail in chapter 5, which presents specific tools for using it to increase confidence.

Acceptance and Commitment Therapy (ACT) expands on the ideas of CBT with a separate mindfulness component that encourages accepting feelings and incorporating personal values in psychological changes. ACT allows for validating negative situations and emotions, rather than denying or dismissing them. This therapy is discussed further in chapter 3.

Exposure Therapy uses relaxation methods while guiding you through the gradual exposure to a particular fear or situation. This exposure slowly increases your confidence by demonstrating that you are safe and in control of your responses. It also decreases the avoidance that often reinforces anxiety. Exposure therapy has been used successfully in treating phobias, post-traumatic stress disorder, and other anxiety disorders. The process of using gradual exposure to combat specific fears and increase confidence is discussed further in chapter 7.

Mindfulness Strategies

Mindfulness can be a useful tool when you are learning to increase your self-confidence and set achievable goals. Mindfulness can decrease feelings of anxiety and being overwhelmed and you can practice it any time and in multiple settings through meditation exercises, relaxation techniques, and grounding techniques. Mindfulness strategies are used in ACT as well as Exposure Therapy.

Meditation exercises: The purpose of these exercises is to clear your mind and relax. Find a few minutes to be completely still and quiet, with limited distractions. Some people find it easiest to practice first thing in the morning or at the end of the day. Set a timer for five minutes. Sit or lie down on your back and place your hands on your knees or stomach. Pay careful attention to your inhale and exhale. Empty your mind of any thoughts or observations. When thoughts do come up (and they will), let them go and return the focus to your breath. This exercise takes time and practice, so be gentle with yourself if you find it difficult. Practice once per day. If you notice that specific thoughts or images continue to come up during meditation, take a moment to write them down in your journal.

Relaxation techniques: Guided imagery exercises can be a wonderful way to relax and decrease anxiety through distraction. Imagine a beautiful location, such as the beach, a mountainside, or a meadow of endless flowers. Place yourself in that location. Imagine what you would smell, what you would see, what you would hear, and how you would feel, physically and emotionally. Be as detailed as possible. Stay in this place for as long as you can. After you end the exercise, write down as much as you can recall about the experience. This will be your script for future relaxation exercises.

Grounding techniques: Grounding techniques bring you back to the present moment, using the specific state of your physical self and environment as a point of reference. If you notice you are feeling overwhelmed and anxious, try redirecting your thoughts to what you see and feel around you. Be as specific as possible, such as, "That chair is red," "I smell coffee," "I hear a dog barking," and "My pen is purple." Pay close attention to how your body is feeling. Notice the weight of your bottom on the chair, the connection between the soles of your feet and the ground, or the feel of your hands on the steering wheel. You can use grounding anytime, anywhere, during any activity.

Setting Achievable Goals

The ability to set goals, and eventually achieve them, is a very important aspect of increasing self-confidence. If your goals are overwhelming or too broad in scope, you will have difficulty achieving them. This can then limit your sense of power. If your goals are specific and have a clear connection to your values, they will be meaningful. Setting small, easily achievable goals and having a specific time frame for completion will set you up for success. The first step is to make sure your goals are as detailed as possible. There are several ways you can accomplish this.

SMART Goals

You can set goals in methodical ways. Although originally designed for goal-setting within the corporate world, the acronym SMART also works in the personal arena. SMART has various interpretations, but it generally stands for Specific, Measurable, Achievable, Realistic, and Timely.

Specific—Your goals must be well defined. "I will begin making healthy choices in my daily life" is not nearly as specific as "I will exercise three days per week. I will stop eating fast food. I will decrease my alcohol intake." The latter set of goals is very specific and therefore increases your likelihood of meeting them.

Measurable—You must have a quantifiable way to measure your progress. Think: numbers. "I am going to exercise for at least 45 minutes three days per week. I will have zero soft drinks. I will drink only one alcoholic beverage per week." If your goals are measurable, you can easily and accurately monitor progress.

Achievable—Your goals should be within your control. Beware of setting goals for activities or situations over which you have limited power. "I will exercise with Brittney" is not an achievable goal if you are depending on Brittney to show up. "I will exercise with Brittney or alone" is better.

Realistic—Your goals should be realistic in terms of your free time and current abilities. If you know you are unlikely to accomplish the goal because it is too overwhelming, do not set it. For example, if you know there is little chance you'll work out every day, adjust the goal to be easier to attain, such as, "I will exercise three days per week."

Timely—Your goal should have a time frame or a projected date of completion. This can be helpful in motivation and planning. You can also set a short-term goal and then assess your next steps, such as, "I will make these changes for the next month and then re-evaluate."

The Importance of Realistic Goals

Remember, do not set overwhelming goals. Instead, set an initial goal you can easily meet, and then increase it over time. For example, if you begin with the goal of exercising three days per week, you can increase it to four days once you have successfully established the benchmark. When you meet your initial goal, your pride and confidence will naturally increase. As your confidence increases, so, too, will the complexity of your goals. Meeting these more complicated goals will contribute to your rising self-confidence.

Values-Driven Goals

Core values are characteristics, ideals, activities, and ways of being that are important to you. They go beyond the expectations of your parents, your teachers, or society at large. They are specific to you and your individual experiences. Take a moment to consider the characteristics you seek out in others. Do you enjoy being around people who are adventurous, wise, or generous? The qualities you look for in others give you a clue about your values. The activities that fill you up and make you feel good about yourself also point toward your values. Maybe you feel amazing after you exercise, attend church, or organize your junk drawer. This could relate to core values of fitness, spirituality, and order. If you enjoy being around friends, making money, and climbing the corporate ladder, this could reflect core values of connection, money, and success.

Values are neither right nor wrong. They are unique and individual. Values influence the ways you interact with your family, community, and workplace. If you value spending time with your family, you are more likely to seek opportunities to be with them. If you value knowledge and learning, you may be more likely to read to your children and get involved in their schoolwork. If you value success and diligence, you are more likely to be very good at your job and spend a great deal of time working.

Values can have different priorities at various times in your life. What is important to you now may not be at the top of the list in a decade. When setting goals, keep your values in mind and make sure your goals reflect them. Be honest about what is important to you. Your goals may represent different values over time, and that is perfectly okay, even expected.

TIPS
Mini Confidence Boosters

The process of building confidence usually includes tiny steps that add up to huge leaps. While you are working on building yourself up, try incorporating one of these mini confidence boosters every day, and notice how much better you feel.

- Wear your favorite outfit—something that makes you feel fabulous.

- Listen to a favorite song.

- Read the autobiography of a confident woman you admire.

- Pamper yourself—get a haircut, massage, or pedicure.

- Do something nice for a stranger—pay for the next customer's coffee in the drive-through, give the waitress a really good tip, or compliment another woman.

- Connect with your spiritual side—say a quick prayer to God, your higher power, the universe, or Mother Nature.

JOURNALING EXERCISE:
Identify Your Goals

Set aside some time to consider and write down your goals for every aspect of your life. Be sure to touch on each of the following categories:

CAREER: Imagine you have the confidence to fully engage your strengths and potential in your professional life. What would this look like? What kind of work would you be doing? What opportunities would you accept, pursue, or even decline? Set some specific, realistic, and values-driven goals.

RELATIONSHIPS: Imagine you have the confidence to be your most authentic self with others. What would this look like? What kinds of people would you attract? What relationships would you need to walk away from? How would this affect boundaries with others? Set some specific and realistic goals that are in line with your values.

PARENTING: Imagine you have the confidence to fully engage with your children and live your values in every aspect of your parenting. What would this look like? What would you need to change in order to accomplish these goals? How would your children respond to these changes?

HEALTH: Imagine you have the confidence to allow your mind and body to be the strongest and most healthy it ever has been. What habits would you need to change to better reflect your values? What realistic goals can you set for yourself to improve your overall wellness? What does your mental health look like when you are in line with your values and goals?

COMMUNITY: Imagine you are confident enough to interact within your community in ways that reflect your values. What does this look like? What opportunities or invitations would you accept or decline? What type of work would you do within your community? Set some specific, realistic, and values-driven goals.

Putting Strategies into Practice

Let's revisit Ashley and see how she implemented these strategies.

Once Ashley recognized that she was unhappy, she began to identify opportunities to increase her happiness. First, she used meditation practices to slow down and clear her mind. She noticed that ideas for stories kept popping up, and she jotted down details in her journal.

Ashley also began to recognize that her current situation was not in line with these personal values. She valued family and intimate relationships, and knew she wanted children. Her current workload was not conducive to meeting someone with whom she could share her life. Ashley wanted to feel successful and proud of herself. She did not want to care so much about others' opinions of her career and life choices. She realized that although she was 26 years old and financially responsible, she was not completely independent from her parents because she continued to push aside her dreams to follow their plans for her life. Ashley came up with the following list of values:

1. Independence
2. Love
3. Creativity
4. Knowledge
5. Success (as I define it)

Ashley knew having the goal to change careers was too overwhelming, and therefore not realistic. She decided to break it down into smaller, more attainable goals. Eventually she came up with the following plan of small steps that were in line with her values:

1. I will decrease my workday to eight hours to allow for a social life. I will no longer bring work home. I will plan one social outing per week.

2. I will continue meditative practices to open my mind to creativity. I will meditate for at least 10 minutes daily.

3. I will spend two hours every Saturday working on a creative writing project.

4. When my parents voice concerns or opinions about my life, I will use clear and kind statements to maintain healthy boundaries.

5. I will evaluate these goals in one month.

After one month of following this plan, Ashley felt more confident. She began submitting her short stories to local publications and reached out to her college creative writing teacher for suggestions. She set new goals for herself that were more complex and in line with her growing self-confidence.

Small, achievable steps can lead to big overall growth over time. Ashley's success and increased confidence is largely attributable to the fact that she did not begin her journey with a broad, overwhelming goal, like "I will change my career and become an author." Her purposeful, strategic, time-limited plan comprising small, realistic goals increased her self-confidence slowly but surely along the way.

PART II
The Strategies

In part 2 you will learn specific techniques for increasing self-confidence. This begins with a cornerstone of Acceptance and Commitment Therapy: acceptance. As discussed in chapter 1, women who have high levels of self-confidence also have high levels of self-esteem, and vice versa. Loving yourself is paramount when working to increase your self-confidence. Accepting yourself as you truly are, not as you represent yourself to the world, is an act of self-love. The more you love yourself, the higher in esteem you will hold yourself, which in turn increases confidence in yourself overall.

This chapter explains how you can nurture physical manifestations of self-confidence, such as mindfulness, physical health, and body language. We will discuss specific recommendations for adjusting your physical state to optimize self-confidence.

We also explore my favorite clinical tool, Cognitive Behavioral Therapy. After you come to understand how your thoughts influence your self-esteem and self-confidence, you will learn how you can change these thoughts to your advantage. You will be empowered to make real changes in your life that will increase confidence in yourself and your abilities.

The final chapter puts all the pieces together to move forward with achieving your primary goal (and your reason for reading this book): increasing your self-confidence.

CHAPTER 3

Practicing Acceptance

When discussing acceptance, it is important to recognize the difference between your strengths and your challenges. Taking this a step further, it's crucial to distinguish between challenges that are in your control to change and those that are not. Acceptance is not an excuse for behaviors that deliberately hurt others or yourself. The challenges in behavior and interactions with the world that affect others (or yourself) in a negative way are within your control to change. This is not the same as accepting them or adopting a mindset of *"That's just the way I am."* On the other hand, when discussing challenges outside your control, like physical characteristics, the goal is to get to a place of acceptance. In this case you are encouraged to adopt a mindset of "That's just the way I am," but with a positive spin on the perceived challenge.

Accepting your strengths can be extremely empowering, especially if you have never allowed yourself to feel pride in or excitement about your gifts and talents. By the end of this chapter, I hope that you have a clear and honest picture of yourself, and that you are able to see yourself as the amazing, talented, complicated, and beautiful woman you are.

Keep in mind that your strengths can lead to challenges. Sometimes the characteristics that help you be successful in one area of your life cause issues in other areas.

Megan, 45, has a career as a paralegal and is married with two preteen sons. She works hard and does a great deal of pro bono work at the local women's shelter for victims of domestic violence. She volunteers for every school bake sale, is very active in her sons' extracurricular activities, and fields constant calls for help and support. Megan is often asked for advice, but she becomes strangely irritated when her advice is not followed. She has a tendency to micromanage at work, often completing tasks that are not her responsibility. She is a caregiver at home, doing all the laundry and making all the appointments, and she never asks her children or husband for help. She does everything for everyone and then feels resentful. She is unable to recognize her role in perpetuating this dynamic. While her husband and sons relax around the house on the weekends, she runs around frantically picking up, refusing to let anyone help but getting aggravated that she is doing everything alone. She rarely takes a moment for herself, claiming she does not have time.

Many people have told Megan that she is too controlling, but she has difficulty accepting that doing everything for everyone does more harm than good. Her micromanaging has caused others to believe that she has no confidence in their abilities. This is especially true for her children. Megan's tendencies to take over and control their behavior has led to a pattern of enabling, which has decreased her children's self-confidence. They are highly anxious and unsure of themselves, which causes friction in Megan's marriage. The constant arguing and blame-setting turns into frustration and anxiety, which perpetuates the controlling behaviors.

Megan has many strengths but also trouble accepting the challenges that have developed as a result of those strengths— namely, her need to control everyone and everything around her. It is possible for strengths to evolve into challenges if not kept in check. It can be difficult to differentiate between the two, especially when those challenges have led to positive results, in the same way Megan's control has led to career success and the ability to help others.

Accepting Your Strengths

Many women struggle to accept their strengths, or even deny them outright. A typical example is responding to a compliment with a self-deprecating comment, like saying, "Oh, it's so dirty!" when someone admires your hair. Or perhaps you haven't raised your hand in class because it would have been the fifth time you answered a question and you did not want others to feel bad about themselves—or think you were full of yourself. Same goes if you tend to put on a "hot mess mama" façade when you are actually naturally organized and highly creative, and require very little sleep to function.

The first step in increasing your self-confidence is identifying and accepting your strengths. This can be an uncomfortable process, especially if you are not accustomed to tooting your own horn, but it is absolutely necessary.

Identify Your Strengths

Many clinicians approach therapy from a strengths-based perspective. Focusing on a client's strengths is key to developing an effective treatment plan. This increases self-confidence, and giving someone goals based on their strengths increases their ability to be successful.

To identify your strengths, consider the opinions of the people who love you. What do your close friends say about you? What do your children say? The people who love you likely think the world of you, and will focus on positives rather than negatives.

Next, think about what you love about yourself. What do you do well? What characteristics make you unique? Think about the values you identified in the previous chapter. Do you embody these values in the ways you interact with others at home, at work, or out in the world? If you cannot come up with your own strengths, refer to the list of what loved ones say, and start there.

Why Do We Downplay Our Strengths?

Why do some women have difficulty accepting compliments, and how does this affect self-confidence? Some women feel uncomfortable with their strengths because they have not fully accepted them, or they lack the confidence to believe the strength even exists. You may not know how to respond to a compliment. A simple "thank you" may feel awkward because you don't want to appear arrogant. You may think the simple act of acknowledging a strength will make someone feel bad about herself, but the only one feeling that way is you. When people comment on your strengths or compliment you, thank them. Even if you have trouble accepting the strength as truth, act *as if* you believe it to be true and have already accepted it. What we say and what we think become mental tape recordings that repeat the same statements over and over. If you are constantly saying, or even thinking, negative things about yourself, those words become your mantras.

When you downplay a strength, you chip away at your confidence. Not only that, but downplaying your strengths also encourages other women to downplay theirs. When you recognize and celebrate your strengths, you give others the confidence to do the same, which is a wonderful thing.

Turn Your Strengths into Positive Mantras

When you turn your strengths into positive self-statements, you start to increase your self-confidence. You will learn more about this practice in chapter 5, but begin by turning your strengths into statements that invoke positive feelings. Use "I am" statements along with the strength ("I am kind," "I am smart," "I am creative," "I am organized"). Or take it a step further and develop a statement that also reflects how your strength helps others ("My creativity brings joy to others around me," "My intelligence allows me to help others by sharing my skills," "My organizational skills make me an efficient and productive employee").

Celebrate Your Strengths

It is an exercise in self-love to recognize your gifts, be grateful for them, and share them with the world. It is not arrogant to know you have talents that others may not possess. It is okay to say, "I am really good at keeping my house organized." If you're the next Marie Kondo, claim it and be proud. If you have a talent for creativity—art, baking, decorating, sewing—accepting and sharing it can help others. If you are a talented surgeon, a great dog trainer, a gifted musician, or an excellent teacher, don't minimize it. Viewing strengths as gifts you can use to better your family, your career, or your community is a way of celebrating them, and ultimately an act of self-love.

It can be challenging to identify your strengths, especially if you are in the habit of discrediting them. Use Megan's inventory as a guide. If you were to ask your partner, your child, or your best friend what they love most about you, what would they say? List their responses as strengths in the first column. In the next column, write down the positive qualities you see in yourself, even if they are already in the first column. Turn these strengths into positive self-statements in the third column. In the final column, state how you can share your strengths with others. Make sure to bookmark this page so you can return and add more strengths that you identify later (because you will!).

MEGAN'S STRENGTHS INVENTORY	
WHAT DO OTHERS SAY ARE MY STRENGTHS?	**WHAT DO I SEE AS MY STRENGTHS?**
Makes good cupcakes	*Good baker*
Generous	*Kind*
Caring	*Caring*
Organized	*Efficient*
TURN THESE INTO POSITIVE SELF-STATEMENTS:	**HOW DO I SHARE THIS WITH THE WORLD?**
1 *"I bake yummy treats with love for my family."*	1 *"I baked cupcakes for our neighbor who just had surgery."*
2 *"I am a generous and kind person with so much to give."*	2 *"I donate my time and volunteer at a women's shelter."*
3 *"I care deeply about others."*	3 *"I show compassion to the women I help at the shelter."*
4 *"I am efficient and productive."*	4 *"I get good results at work, and my organized nature leads to decreased clutter at home."*

Accepting Your Weaknesses

Accepting your weaknesses also leads to growth, change, and a greater understanding of yourself. In order to grow, some discomfort is necessary. When you are able to be honest with yourself about your mistakes and your shortcomings, you are taking the first step in building your self-confidence. Identifying your weaknesses is not about tearing yourself down. It's about accepting who you are while acknowledging areas where you may need some growth and change. Self-confidence grows out of becoming the best version of yourself, and loving yourself through the process.

Identify Your Challenges

For many women, identifying flaws in yourself may be relatively easy, especially when looking at physical characteristics. This is unfortunate, but it highlights some of the factors affecting self-confidence that were discussed in chapter 1. Rather than focusing on the physical characteristics you see as weaknesses, concentrate on your challenges. These may be related to your personality or behavior, your usual ways of interacting with others, or your methods of reacting to negative or positive events.

Once you've identified challenges and weaknesses, you can take steps to deal with them, even as you acknowledge they may never completely disappear. Acceptance comes from loving yourself despite these weaknesses, and self-confidence grows from your ability to view challenges in a more positive light. Self-confidence also grows from your determination to improve qualities that are in your control to change.

Megan's work to identify her challenges looks like this:

MEGAN'S CHALLENGES INVENTORY		
WHAT ARE MY CHALLENGES?	**IS THIS IN MY CONTROL TO CHANGE?**	**ARE THERE ANY POSITIVE SIDES TO THIS CHALLENGE?**
My nose is too big.	No	My nose is something I inherited from my beautiful grandmother.
I eat too much junk food.	Yes	I do not deprive myself of treats.
I'm controlling.	Yes	I am organized, efficient, and helpful.
I worry too much.	Yes	I care deeply about the people I love and want them to be safe.

Recognizing the positive aspects of your challenges, especially those that are not in your capacity to change (i.e., physical traits), allows you to practice loving and accepting yourself. Loving yourself and seeing your challenges in a positive light increases your self-confidence.

When you recognize the challenges in your control to change, you acknowledge the complexities of your nature and remember you have the power to change your reactions, responses, and habits. Begin the work of identifying ways you can improve upon your challenges, and turn these into goals using the tips from chapter 2. At the end of this chapter, you will see how Megan developed goals by recognizing weaknesses that were in her control to improve.

Adopt a Growth Mindset

A growth mindset is vital to maintaining positivity through challenges, as you are able to look at possibilities rather than just accept things as they are. Try to see your talents as gifts that you can develop rather than innate, fixed concepts. Accept that change is possible—and unavoidable.

When you shift to a growth mindset, you start to take in feedback with the understanding that it is not personal, and you will view setbacks as opportunities for improvement and growth. Instead of beating yourself up for mistakes, you'll embrace them as part of the process and learn to value your own tenacity.

Adopting a growth mindset leads you to approach your personal challenges with excitement because you know change is possible. You are not stuck with your weaknesses or powerless to change your behavior.

Make Mistakes

Mistakes are part of living and growing. Avoid using them as an excuse to give up or a reason to feel guilty. Learning from your mistakes can be an exercise in self-confidence because you now know what not to do. The more experiences you have, whether successes or failures, the more you understand yourself.

Have you ever made a mistake that ended up becoming the best thing that ever happened to you, either because of the lesson you learned or the changes you made as a result? If we quit every time we experienced failure, we would never learn to walk, talk, read, write, or do anything, really. Failure leads to growth. Keep your expectations of yourself realistic. You are not perfect, and you were not intended to be. Practice viewing each mistake as a necessary stepping-stone to where you are meant to be and who you are meant to become.

Practice Self-Compassion

Self-compassion is the act of giving yourself grace to make mistakes, be wrong, and have weaknesses. Accept that you are human and imperfect, and it is okay. It is often easier to have compassion for others while holding yourself to impossible standards. Recognize that you, too, deserve compassion, forgiveness, and love and respect—especially when you are not perfect.

Next time you're being especially hard on yourself, ask yourself what you would say to your best friend in this situation. Chances are, your response would be full of understanding, encouragement, and love. So why would you tell yourself anything less?

You are your own worst critic. Have empathy for yourself. Recognize you are doing the best you can with your given circumstances. Recognize that some things are in your control, and others are not. Make a plan to move forward on the things you can improve, and acknowledge and accept the rest.

THOUGHT EXERCISE:
Compassion for Yourself

Are you struggling to find compassion for something in particular? Think of a time when you were unnecessarily hard on yourself. Maybe you hurt someone without intending to. Maybe you made an error at work that had terrible consequences. Maybe you became frustrated and yelled at your children. No matter how awful the mistake, recognize that you deserve forgiveness. Write this down: "I am imperfect and deserving of forgiveness." List the ways you have grown and learned from the mistake. Then let it go.

Strategies you can use right now to help you stay in a growth mindset:

- Take a compliment with grace by simply saying "thank you." Or, if you feel the need to add more, you can say, "Thank you! That is kind of you to say," or "I really appreciate that."

- Give out compliments freely and honestly, especially to other women.

- Use the positive self-statements developed in the strengths exercise earlier in this chapter, and say them out loud frequently. Write some on sticky notes that you can see throughout your day.

- Practice compassion. Be kind to yourself. Say out loud, "I am doing the best I can right now, and that is okay."

- Each week, using your strengths inventory, choose one way to share your strengths with the world.

- Tell someone three things that went well for you this week. Invite her to tell you three things that went well in her life as well.

Putting Strategies into Practice

Let's revisit Megan and see how she implemented these strategies.

Megan's husband encourages her to see a counselor. She knows she does not want to lose her marriage, and she realizes she needs to try to make some changes. Through her work with the therapist, Megan identifies the source of her need to control, and develops self-compassion. When the therapist gently points out the ways in which Megan has contributed to the family's turmoil, she does not become defensive or see this as criticism. Instead, she accepts that she has made mistakes. She recognizes she made many of these mistakes because she had the misguided idea she was responsible for the happiness of others.

Once Megan fills out her self-awareness inventories, she is able to fully understand how her strengths and challenges have helped and hurt her. She adopts a growth mindset and decides to improve on the challenges over which she has control. She recognizes that her strength of caring for others is also a weakness when she does not allow others to do things for themselves. She understands how her tendency to enable her children has hindered their abilities to develop self-confidence. She learns that feeling resentful is a red flag, warning her that she is doing too much for others and needs to take a step back. She begins to make self-care a priority, which helps curb her junk-food habit. Using the tips from chapter 2, Megan is able to make specific goals to improve her tendency to control, her eating habits, and her anxiety.

Megan's self-confidence grows alongside her understanding of herself. She comes to accept her positive and negative qualities. Knowing she has some control over her challenging characteristics and seeing concrete improvements give her the motivation to continue moving forward.

CHAPTER 4

Embodying Self-Confidence

Confidence is not just related to your thought processes. Your physical state is also important in cultivating a healthy mindset for practicing self-confidence. You may have heard of the mind–body connection, which is the idea that if you are in a healthy physical state, it is easier to reach a healthy mental state, and vice versa. The same is true of confidence. When you emanate confidence through your physical state, you will feel more confident mentally. And a confident mindset leads to corresponding body language, posture, and gestures.

Maintaining your physical health makes you feel good, which spreads to other areas of your life. Taking care of your mind and body reinforces the idea that you deserve that care and concern, and are worth the extra effort and attention, which goes a long way in developing self-confidence. The emotional benefits of physical self-care can be just as significant.

The way others perceive your confidence influences how they interact with you, which in turn gives you feedback that can either reinforce or decrease your self-confidence. The ways you nurture your appearance and physical state can reflect your inner self and send positive messages to the world. Self-confidence affects the silent ways you express yourself though body language, posture, and eye contact.

Beth, 28, suffers from an extreme lack of self-confidence. Although she is highly intelligent and very kind, she approaches people and situations expecting that she will be disliked and will fail. She is overweight and dresses in large, baggy clothing to conceal her body. She is in the habit of eating fast food and she has not been to the doctor for a wellness visit in a couple of years. She frequently stays up too late and oversleeps the next day. Her effort in her appearance has diminished, as she no longer bothers to fix her hair or apply makeup. She often focuses on the negative side of things, and others avoid speaking with her at work because she is always complaining. This reinforces her belief that she is not liked, but she is unable to recognize that others are responding to her negativity and lack of self-confidence, rather than her true self.

It can be difficult to know which comes first—decreased self-confidence, which leads to lack of self-care, or lack of self-care, which leads to decreased self-confidence. Whichever the case, your physical state will always influence how you feel about yourself and the ways in which you present yourself to the world. You can begin implementing habits and practices to embody self-confidence, and you'll see how these small changes can influence your sense of self and overall happiness.

Practicing Mindfulness

As discussed in chapter 2, practicing mindfulness has numerous benefits. It helps quiet your mind and keep you in the present rather than obsessing about the past or worrying about the future. When you stop thinking about what has already happened or not yet occurred, you are able to focus on what is in your control. This includes your behavior, reactions, decisions, and thoughts.

Mindfulness goes beyond simple meditation practices. It helps you stay in the here and now, which is useful in keeping a healthy physical state. Being centered and aware of your physical self allows you to adjust your posture or body language. It also leads to improved attention toward your basic needs for nutritious food and adequate sleep. Being mindful of your dialogue and unspoken thoughts can give you good insight into those tape recordings of old, unhelpful messages that lead to roadblocks in improving your self-confidence. Mindfulness is extremely useful in keeping your negative thoughts in check.

Mindfulness Basics

The primary goal of mindfulness is remaining aware of yourself—your mood, physical state, thoughts, and behavior—in your present moment.

You can achieve a mindful state anywhere, at any time. Getting into this state does not take much time, but staying there requires practice. Just like with any other good habit, becoming mindful requires repetition.

STRATEGIES

Try these quick activities to bring you back to the present.

- Use your guided imagery exercise from chapter 2 to get into a state of peace and relaxation. Close your eyes and immerse yourself completely in this environment, paying close attention to the smells, sounds, and feelings it invokes. Then gently bring yourself back to the present moment. Use this as a reset button whenever you need to bring yourself to a place of calmness.

- Be completely still for one minute. Set a timer if needed. Do not move at all—not even to scratch an itch—except to breathe. See how hard this is to do. Focus on how your body feels in this moment. Concentrate on your breathing. Pay attention to any thoughts that come up. Practice being attuned to your unspoken thoughts, as well as the words you use to express yourself. This will be very helpful in identifying negative patterns of thought.

- Take a moment to tune in to your body. Are you tense? Do you need to use the bathroom? When was the last time you drank water or ate something? Relax anything that is twitching or tight. Take care of your basic physical needs, then refocus on the current task.

- Briefly focus on your body language, assessing what you are conveying to others. How is your posture? Are your arms crossed? Are you frowning? Adjust accordingly.

Practicing Relaxation

Practicing relaxation takes time and patience. It can take a while to feel comfortable or familiar. Give yourself patience and grace, and let go of the idea of doing it perfectly. Continue your practice. People who practice relaxation report an overall sense of calm and well-being. Relaxation also gives you the quiet you need to clear your mind and allow positive thoughts and energy to flow in. Before you begin a relaxation or meditation exercise, briefly reflect on something that has been making you unhappy or decreasing your self-confidence. Having a clear mind throughout your relaxation practice keeps you open to potential solutions.

If you want guidance in your relaxation exercises, there are useful apps you can use to provide prompts (see Resources, page 115). The basic methods are outlined below.

Deep Breathing

Your breath is your life force. Focusing on your breathing is a primary relaxation strategy. It helps you become centered so you can ignore outside distractions and focus on your body and inner self. Inner focus allows you the space to reflect on how you're feeling in the moment. To begin, get into a seated comfortable position or lie down on your back. Take deep breaths in and out of your nose. Feel the breath enter your nose, fill your lungs, and come back out. Each inhalation and exhalation is one count. Focus on breathing and counting. If thoughts come up, keep returning to your breath.

Muscle Relaxation

Practicing muscle relaxation can be useful when you are tense or having trouble sleeping. When you focus on all the different aspects of your body, you'll have a greater appreciation for what it can do. Begin by contracting and clenching all the muscles in your body, from your toes to your face. Hold for a few seconds,

then very slowly release each muscle one by one, beginning with your toes and gradually moving upward. Sink into yourself and feel the weight of your body succumb to gravity. Repeat until you feel relaxed. Recognize how powerful your body is, and all the amazing intricacies that come together to make you the woman you are.

Practicing Gratitude

Focusing on things that are good can have an impact on your overall positivity. It can be so easy to turn our attention to what is bad, scary, or wrong with the world, and social media does not help. Take the time to change that narrative. Even if you are able to find only a few small things to be grateful for today, start there. If you have eyes that can see, a comfortable place to sleep, and people you love, that's a good place to start.

Gratitude Statements

Expressing gratitude can be an incredibly simple but effective way of bringing more joy into your life. Each morning, when you wake up or on your commute to work, state three things for which you are grateful. For example:

- I am grateful for the sun.

- I am grateful for books to read.

- I am grateful for my feet, which are strong enough to hold my weight.

These are your gratitude statements for the day. If you are feeling especially grateful, expand the list. The more you focus on the positive, the more good you will see in the world. The more things you express gratitude for, the more you will find to be grateful for. There is nothing too small or insignificant—think traffic lights, the rain, your morning coffee, music, your children, the color blue. The same things will likely come up again and again, but try to mix it up.

Once you are in the habit of expressing gratitude every morning, begin writing your gratitude statements in a notebook. When you're having a difficult day, look at what you've written. Remind yourself of the gratitude. Bring yourself back to a mindful place where you are able to see all this goodness. Encourage your children, your partner, and your friends to begin this practice, and spread this gratitude to everyone you love. Watch how this begins to transform your outlook.

Being Aware of Body Language

Stand up straight. Don't slouch. Make eye contact. Yes, I sound like your mom. But it's absolutely true that you will feel more capable and confident if you take the effort to put your best foot forward. This includes posture, gestures, eye contact, facial expressions, and other nonverbal methods of communicating. Body language and the way you present yourself to the world make a difference in how others perceive you and how you feel about yourself, both of which affect your confidence.

Posture

To appear open and approachable, stand up straight and tall, avoid crossing your arms across your chest, and make good eye contact. This posture conveys a sense of confidence, and people are more likely to believe what you say and take you seriously if you are directly engaged with them. Even if you are not feeling particularly confident, act as though you are, and see how this simple practice influences your interactions.

Power Poses

The Wonder Woman pose is not just for little kids and super-heroes. Though it may seem (and feel) ridiculous, standing with your feet planted firmly and apart, fists on hips, and chin raised can invoke feelings of power and confidence.

Power poses, a term first used by Harvard professors in a 2012 study, have been controversial among researchers but widely accepted by the mainstream as a method for increasing feelings of control in situations that cause a person to feel helpless. Any pose that is open and expansive can be considered a power pose. Another common one is to put your arms in a V for Victory and plant your feet widely apart. Try one of these poses before an interview, a first date, or a big sales pitch, and pay attention to any feelings it invokes.

Your Appearance

Do not underestimate the power of making an effort with your physical appearance. Taking a few extra minutes in the morning to get dressed, brush your hair, or apply a small amount of makeup can make a difference in how you feel throughout the day. Wear clean, unwrinkled clothes. Lay out your outfit the night before if that helps you with your morning routine. If you feel and look more put-together, you will have more confidence in your interactions, and others will respond to your positive vibes. Try doing just one little thing each day. Whether you are a stay-at-home mom or a corporate executive, you deserve a little boost in your confidence.

Facial Expressions

Pay attention to your facial expressions. Are your emotions usually written all over your face? If others can always tell what you're thinking and feeling, be careful about how this can influence your interactions, especially when you are angry or upset. If you are trying to increase confidence, especially in the work environment, pay close attention to your facial cues. If your brow is furrowed and you are frowning, this conveys that you are unhappy, angry, or irritated. If you want to convey a negative message, such as to your partner or your misbehaving child, that is absolutely acceptable.

Being able to express yourself honestly with the people closest to you is important, and feeling safe enough to do so is a vital reflection of intimacy and connection. If you are in a place where this nonverbal language does not serve you well, however, such as the office, your child's school, or on a date, practice some deep breathing, relax your face muscles, and smile. This is not to say you must be concerned about what others think about you, but their interactions with you can reinforce negative beliefs you have about yourself, which you will learn how to tackle in chapter 5. Your nonverbal cues influence the feedback you receive from others, which can contribute to your overall mood and self-confidence, much like Beth at the beginning of this chapter.

Smiling is known to increase happiness. Practice smiling even if you're not feeling happy. Think of something funny. Search for animal videos on YouTube. Do a silly dance in your living room. Tell your kids "My best friend in the whole wide world is a hippo named Boo-Boo Butt" (thank you, *The Book with No Pictures*). Jot down some funny memories to have on hand when you're not feeling happy. Read your gratitude journal.

Maintaining Physical Health

Taking care of your physical health is a necessity, and not something to place at the end of your to-do list. Humans need food, water, sleep, and exercise to maintain a healthy weight, fight off germs and illnesses, and have the energy to work and play. You also need good boundaries and self-care to allow yourself the space and permission to do things that make you feel good about yourself. You are a multifaceted person with emotional and physical needs. Caring for yourself as a whole leads to increased happiness and self-confidence. Neglect of any of these areas can lead to illness, overwhelm, and decreased self-confidence. If you are not taking care of yourself, you are sending a message to yourself and others that you are not worth the effort and your body and physical health are not important.

Let's look at how you can flip this narrative, and work toward building your confidence from the inside out.

Sleep

Our bodies need sleep to recharge. Sleep deprivation is linked to anxiety, obesity, and other health problems. Proper sleep is a necessity. Getting too much sleep can be detrimental to your mood and physical state. If you are not sleeping well because you are unable to fall asleep easily or you wake up in the middle of the night, try the mindfulness and relaxation exercises discussed earlier in the chapter.

Other helpful sleep tips include:

- Go to bed around the same time every night.

- Wake up at the same time every morning.

- Avoid alcohol and caffeine in the afternoon and evening.

- Avoid screen time within an hour before bedtime.

- Take a relaxing bath before bedtime.

- Keep a notebook at your bedside where you can jot down any thoughts that worry you, tasks to add to your to-do list, or anything else that comes up.

If you have tried everything but are still having difficulties, speak with your health care provider. Sleep issues can be linked to underlying physical and mental health issues that require professional treatment.

Exercise

Exercise is one of the most underused treatments for depression and anxiety. The benefits of exercise are numerous for physical as well as mental health.

Many women have vitamin D deficiency, which can lead to symptoms of depression and anxiety. You can remedy this by spending more time outdoors. You can add exercise to your life in simple ways—taking the stairs, parking in the rear of the parking lot, or walking the dog. Sign up for free home-exercise routines online. Purchase a used treadmill or exercise equipment for your home. Sign up for exercise programs at a community center or a local gym. So many options exist for every income and fitness level. Do some research and find something that works for you. Keep in mind the strategies for setting realistic goals as discussed in chapter 2.

If you already have a good exercise routine going, step outside your comfort zone and try something new to keep you engaged and motivated.

Eating Healthfully

You put out what you put in. If you are filling your amazing body with junk and fast food, you will feel sluggish and unmotivated. Give your body the nutrients it needs to function well. Treat yourself, but pay attention to your input and make sure your food choices are balanced.

Meal planning and advanced meal preparation can be helpful, and there are so many tips and tricks and menus online. Many food service companies have ready-made healthy meals you can purchase. Incorporate whatever works best for you and your family.

Talk to your health care provider about whether you need to take a multivitamin, omega-3s, probiotics, or any other supplement. Increase your daily water intake, and limit soft drinks and alcohol.

Basic Self-Care and Hygiene

Caring for your body's most basic needs gives you the energy to be healthy and sets the foundation for building confidence. This may seem like a simple concept, but when you are feeling bad about yourself and your confidence is low, it is easy to put basic care on the back burner. Resist this urge. Wash your hair, floss your teeth, go to the gynecologist for your annual Pap smear, and schedule that mammogram. Wear sunscreen. Moisturize. Drink water. Paint your toenails. Put your physical health and self-care at the top of your priority list, because that is what you deserve.

Be aware of boundaries. Are you giving too much of yourself and neglecting self-care? Practice saying *no* more frequently, especially when you are feeling overwhelmed. Remember that you don't have to take care of everyone around you, and you can also ask for help when you need it. Figure out what gives you energy and motivation, whether it's spending time alone or with others, and do it as often as possible. This could be a bubble bath with a good book, a date night with your partner, a shopping trip with friends, a massage, prayer, or whatever fills you up. Just as your body needs physical care and attention, so does your emotional and spiritual state. Taking breaks is a crucial aspect of self-care.

STRATEGIES

Begin using these strategies for getting into the best mindset for embodying self-confidence.

- When entering an unfamiliar situation or group of people, act as if you are feeling confident. Smile and make eye contact. Stand up straight and tall. Resist the urge to cross your arms. When you speak with someone, face them straight on rather than turning away.

- Spend 15 extra minutes on your appearance so you are as neat and put-together as possible.

- Try to incorporate 90 minutes of exercise into your week. If you already exercise this much, change up your usual activities—walk in a different neighborhood, try a different exercise program, or invite a friend to join you.

- Begin your gratitude journal. Repeat your statements "I am grateful for . . ." throughout the day.

- Practice the Wonder Woman power pose in the bathroom. Take a moment to giggle if you need to, but stay in the pose.

- Use the healthy sleep tips. Keep a sleep schedule, even on weekends.

- Make your annual gynecologist and wellness appointments if you have not done so this year. Schedule any necessary examinations, blood work, and a mammogram. While you're at it, schedule a dentist appointment, too, along with any other specialists, such as an eye doctor or dermatologist. Put your health at the top of the priority list.

- Schedule breaks, even if it is just a weekend morning at home. Give yourself permission to leave the dishes and laundry to tackle later. Nothing bad will happen if you don't do everything right this minute.

Putting Strategies into Practice

Let's revisit Beth and see how she implemented these strategies.

Beth begins by scheduling an appointment with her gynecologist for a physical exam, a Pap smear, and blood work. Her doctor encourages her to begin a regimen of walking three days per week and provides a handout of tips for healthy eating. On her way home, Beth stops at the grocery store and buys fresh, healthy food. She realizes how worried she had been about not having her Pap smear, and feels so much relief that it's out of the way.

Beth begins her gratitude practice. At first it is difficult because she has trouble finding things to be grateful for. But her list slowly grows. She decides to reconnect with her faith, and makes an effort to pray every day.

Beth also implements new strategies at work. During her morning commute, she focuses on her gratitude statements rather than negative events. She stands up tall, makes eye contact, and smiles more. She goes to bed by 10 p.m. every night and sets her alarm for 6 a.m., even on weekends. She goes for walks in the evenings, then practices relaxation exercises 15 minutes before bed. She plays upbeat music in the bathroom and dances while getting dressed for work. She does not wear makeup, but the simple act of fixing her hair and wearing clean, unwrinkled clothes gives her a boost.

Beth has learned how powerful these small changes can be. Others around her have noticed the shift in her mood, and have begun to include her in conversations and after-work activities. This has increased her confidence and reinforced these changes. Over time, these practices become habits for Beth, leading to continued improvements in her physical health, emotional well-being, and overall confidence.

Now that you are aware of tips on embodying self-confidence and focusing on your physical state and nonverbal communication, let's focus inward, on your thoughts and beliefs.

CHAPTER 5

Reframing Negative Thoughts

This chapter focuses on the nature of negative thoughts and how they can affect your self-confidence. Reframing these thoughts is an important part of changing your inner narrative, which leads you to accept yourself, improves your mindset, and increases your self-esteem and confidence.

For as long as she can remember, Sarah, 27, has been critical of her physical appearance and very hard on herself. She learned from a young age that as the oldest of three children, she was the responsible and capable one. This was reinforced by the stress caused by her middle sibling's special needs. Sarah learned that she received the most attention from her parents when she made good grades and helped out around the house, reinforcing the messaging that B was an unacceptable grade and putting herself first was not rewarding. As a result, Sarah's anxiety was very high throughout high school. She put a great deal of pressure on herself to earn straight As and make things as easy as possible for her parents. She internalized the good-girl label.

Sarah's anxiety and stress followed her to college, where she had a few close friends, kids who were like-minded and responsible. Sarah realized at a young age that she was gay, but she never dated. She lacked the confidence to tell her parents or seek out romantic relationships. She spent most of her free time studying or going home to check on her parents and siblings, who adored her. She gained a great deal of weight while in school, which only reinforced her negative feelings of shame and unhappiness.

Once Sarah was out of school, she launched her career and slowly became more social. She still put others' needs before her own, worried about her parents and siblings, and maintained low self-confidence in her physical appearance and her abilities, even though others frequently complimented her work. She had her first romantic partner, but her caretaking tendencies and need for constant reassurance eventually led to the end of the relationship.

When Sarah returns to graduate school, she decides to begin therapy to help her heal from the breakup. She quickly realizes there is more to her unhappiness, and begins the inner work of identifying the roots of her anxiety and low self-esteem.

Sarah's story illustrates how negative beliefs can reinforce low self-confidence. Sarah's negative thoughts about her physical appearance and her abilities, as well as messages learned in childhood, contribute to her low opinion of herself. We will revisit her story later and learn how she was able to reframe these thoughts to improve her self-esteem.

Negative Thinking and Self-Talk

Negative thinking can be divided into five main categories, although overlap is possible. The following categories include examples of negative statements I frequently hear from my clients.

Negative Thoughts about Your Appearance

I am unattractive. I am fat. I am ugly. I'm gross. My hair never looks good. Clothes never fit right.

All women experience these thoughts from time to time. It's hard to avoid them, especially when you factor in messages from social media and the entertainment industry. As discussed in chapter 1, these messages shape how you feel about your physical appearance. As an adult, it is important to recognize that marketing is marketing, real is real, and fake is fake. Holding yourself to impossible standards is not healthy. Taking good care of yourself—physically and emotionally—by following the suggestions in chapter 4 will help you maintain healthy thoughts about your appearance. Put aside all the unreasonable expectations and pressure and focus on what makes you feel good about yourself.

If you absorbed negative messages about your body at a young age—whether from the media, your family members, or peers—recognize that you can challenge and reframe them. You owe it to yourself to come to a place of love and acceptance of traits over which you have no control, and this cognitive work can help you get there.

Negative Thoughts about Your Capabilities

I can't handle this. I always sound like an idiot. Why would anyone hire me? I am so stupid. I'm a mess.

You are a strong, capable woman. The fact that you are reading this book proves that on some level, you know you are capable of making real changes. Many women downplay their capabilities and intelligence for various reasons. Perhaps you don't want to make others feel bad about themselves. Maybe you believe women are supposed to be pretty, not smart, or that being smart is threatening or unattractive. Maybe you received messaging that led you to believe you were not smart or capable. Some women allow unreasonably high expectations to dictate their perception of competence at home and at work, which leads to feelings of discouragement. Or they believe they cannot, or should not, have to ask for help, which contributes to decreased confidence in their abilities to handle everything. The good news is you have the power to change these negative thoughts.

Negative Thoughts about Your Responsibilities

Helping others is more important than helping myself. I can't say no. I don't want to hurt anyone's feelings. I feel like a bad person if I'm not doing for others. I have to do it all. I shouldn't put my needs first. They need me. If I don't take care of it, who will?

Women, especially mothers, are generally viewed as caretakers. Women are amazing creatures, capable of multitasking that men can only dream of—*call the vet, Sally needs new shoes, there's a dress day at school tomorrow, Ben has a soccer game*

Saturday, make dentist appointments, call the exterminator. This caretaking often spills over to other areas (and people) beyond the home. In my practice, I frequently see women who are constantly doing for others, being emotionally available for adult friends and family members, and taking on more responsibility than they should. Although it is important to be a good friend, daughter, and sister, be sure to balance this with the proper amount of care and concern for yourself.

It is important to recognize when you are doing more than you should for someone else. You cannot help people who don't want to help themselves, and it's not your responsibility to make life easier for everyone around you. Make sure you are clear on what is and is not your responsibility. You should not worry about someone else's consequences more than they do. Most important, you cannot pour from an empty pitcher. Your reserves must be replenished. This is especially hard for women who have always been considered responsible and capable. It's so easy to do for others when you are good at it. But this can also lead to resentment and feeling overwhelmed, especially if your needs are not being met.

Even in parenting, there comes a time when you must step back and allow your child to make mistakes and learn about personal responsibility and consequences. It is not always your job to clear the way, although I know this is much easier said than done.

If you notice yourself getting caught up in someone else's dramas, mistakes, decision-making, or negative consequences, remind yourself of this phrase: "Not my circus, not my monkeys." To understand more about this, consult the Resources (page 115) for recommendations on books related to codependency.

Negative Thoughts about How Others View You

People don't like me. People think I'm unattractive. People think I'm boring. He's so amazing—why is he with me?
Some of the most amazing, fascinating, smart women I have ever had the privilege of working with have shared these

negative thoughts in session. These statements couldn't be further from the truth. A decrease in self-esteem and self-confidence leads women to make these assumptions—and to even care about what others think in the first place. Most people are too caught up in their own emotional storms to be overly concerned with you. Assuming that others feel negatively toward you can change your behavior around them, and it really doesn't matter in the grand scheme as long as you are happy with yourself. Not everyone will like you, and that's okay. If someone doesn't like you, it has much more to do with that person's issues rather than with you.

In relationships, a perceived imbalance between the partners in terms of attractiveness, intelligence, or success can be especially damaging. The need for reassurance from a romantic partner often becomes tiring. If your partner says they love you exactly as you are, believe them. Entertaining negative thoughts about your worthiness will only lead to more pain and drama. Identifying and changing these negative beliefs can improve not only your confidence in yourself, but also your confidence within your relationships.

Negative Thoughts Learned in Childhood

It is not okay to talk about my feelings. Keeping up appearances is more important than being honest. It is not safe to discuss bad things that happened in my family. I must agree with my parents. I am a disappointment. I have to be the responsible one.

I saved the most damaging, and the most pervasive, for last. Negative thoughts learned in childhood are tricky to identify and challenge because you often hold them so deep in your subconscious and have been carrying them around such a long time.

All families have rules. Some, such as no running with scissors or making your bed every morning, are healthy. Others are not. In much of my work with women, when we get to the root of their self-esteem or self-confidence struggles, we end up discussing their childhoods and the messages they received before they were old enough to know better.

This is especially true for women who were victims of abuse or grew up with addicts, alcoholics, or emotionally unavailable parents—or both. Children in these environments frequently receive the messages that their voices and feelings are not important, that the people who are supposed to love and protect them will fail to do so, that walking on eggshells is necessary to keep the peace. Rewriting these negative thoughts can be some of the hardest inner work you will ever do, but it is also the most rewarding, not just for yourself, but also for future generations.

In cases such as childhood abuse or living with an alcoholic parent, I highly recommend doing this work with the help and support of a licensed therapist. See the Resources (page 115) for more information on choosing a therapist.

JOURNAL EXERCISE:
Identify Your Negative Thoughts

Reflect on the negative thoughts discussed in this section. How did you feel while you were reading them? Did any seem familiar? Write down the one that resonated with you most. How has this negative thought influenced how you feel about yourself? Over the next week, monitor your thoughts and note when this negative thought comes to mind. Observe your confidence levels at those times. How does one influence the other?

Putting an End to Negative Thoughts

Negative thoughts are pervasive. Whether you learned them from the adults in your life or came up with them on your own, they can easily take over your feelings and emotions. Much like a wheelbarrow forming a rut in the route it follows over and over, negative thoughts create pathways in our brain that become so automatic they can be difficult to recognize. But once you are aware of their existence, it is easier to identify them and stop them in their tracks. Remember, you have the power to change your mindset by using the same process that caused the negative feelings in the first place. This is the basis for Cognitive Behavioral Therapy, as discussed in chapter 2.

Identify Negative Thoughts

Identifying negative thoughts is the first step in ending them. Negative thoughts usually come up when you are overwhelmed, resentful, angry, guilty, embarrassed, scared, or sad: *I can't believe I just said that, I'm such an idiot, I shouldn't need help, Other women handle this better than I do, I'm a terrible wife/partner/mother, I always have to do everything around here, My hair never looks good.*

Sounds familiar, right?

Most women have negative thoughts about themselves, their capabilities, their intelligence, and their physical appearance at some point, but when these thoughts are allowed to take over, it can lead to decreased self-confidence and low self-esteem. The opposite is true for emotions like happiness, excitement, contentment, and pride. These feelings generally go along with positive thoughts, such as *I really did a great job with that project, This dress looks awesome on me, I am doing the best I can and that is okay.* These thoughts lead to more confidence and self-acceptance.

When you are experiencing a strong feeling, whether positive or negative, there are accompanying thoughts. Pay careful attention to your mood and emotions throughout the day. When you are feeling negative emotions, stop and ask yourself the following questions:

1. What am I doing at this moment? (driving to work, cooking dinner, shopping for a dress, scrolling through Facebook)

2. How am I feeling? (aggravated, sad, discouraged, overwhelmed)

3. What am I telling myself about the situation or the feeling itself?

It can be helpful to write these thoughts and feelings in a notebook or quickly type them into your phone so you can review them later. This will become your thought record. Thought records are important because your negative thoughts tend to repeat themselves, and it is helpful to recognize your patterns.

This may feel difficult at first. Identifying negative thoughts takes practice. Most of us are not accustomed to evaluating our thoughts so intensely; instead, we are too focused on feeling and reacting. But this process becomes automatic. Before you know it, the questions *What am I thinking right now? Why am I feeling like this?* will be integrated into your day.

Let's go back to Sarah, now in therapy for treatment of anxiety and low self-esteem. For homework, Sarah's therapist asked her to fill out the following thought record prior to her next session.

WHAT AM I DOING?	WHAT AM I FEELING?	WHAT AM I THINKING?
Getting dressed for dinner with friends.	Shame, sadness	I am fat and ugly.
Working on a research project for school.	Overwhelmed, discouraged	This project has to be perfect. I'll never finish in time.
Driving home to visit parents and siblings.	Resentful, overwhelmed	I have to help my family. They need me. I'm the responsible one.

Notice that Sarah's feelings are the result of her thoughts, and the more she has these thoughts, the stronger the feelings are.

If every time she gets dressed—whether for work, for a party, or just to run errands on the weekend—she is thinking negative thoughts, they will continue to reinforce her negative feelings. The negative feelings will seep into other areas of her life, decreasing her self-worth and self-confidence.

But she can change this internal narrative, and so can you.

Reframe Negative Self-Talk

Once you can identify your negative thoughts, you can begin the process of reframing them into more positive, helpful thoughts. Let's look at how Sarah's thoughts might be reframed:

NEGATIVE THOUGHT	REFRAMED THOUGHT
I am fat and ugly.	*I am a beautiful, interesting person, with people who love me exactly as I am.*
This has to be perfect.	*I'm doing my best, and that is enough.*
I'll never finish in time.	*I will take this one section at a time, and it will get done.*
I have to help my family.	*I can help my family by helping myself first.*
They need me.	*They are adults and responsible for themselves.*
I'm the responsible one.	*I am not responsible for the happiness of others.*

You can reframe any negative thought. If you are struggling to come up with your own, maybe one of these will resonate:

- I have many gifts to share with others.

- I am strong and brave.

- I do not have to do it all right now.

- I have the power to change my circumstances.

- Done is better than perfect.

- It is okay to ask for help.

- I can make a plan to help me feel better about this.

Quiet Your Inner Critic

If you are not paying attention, your negative thoughts tend to become mantras that repeat in your head and shape your reality. These thoughts become an inner critic that lies to you, saying you are not worthy, not capable, not lovable. These damaging self-statements become ingrained beliefs about yourself, and they can take over. Using positive, reframed statements can slowly quiet that inner critic and transform it into a healthy, supportive, encouraging voice.

Reinforce Your Healthy Inner Voice

You've likely heard of constructive criticism, or the idea that focusing on strengths while giving feedback leads to important and necessary change. Your inner critic is not in and of itself a bad guy. Sometimes it is helpful to critique your behavior, work, or decisions, especially if it leads to growth and personal accountability.

It is important, however, to make sure your inner critic is healthy and kind, a constructive voice that encourages you to do better. If this voice expresses only negative ideas, you will quickly become defeated and unsure of yourself.

Your inner voice should speak to you like a best friend who loves you exactly as you are, faults and all. Someone who wants you to succeed and be happy. What should Sarah's kind inner voice be saying to her—the negative thoughts or the reframed thoughts? Which are more helpful in increasing Sarah's self-esteem?

Obviously, the correct answer is reframed thoughts. You can make sure your inner voice stays healthy, holds you accountable when necessary, and above all gives you unconditional positive regard by giving it a steady stream of positive mantras to pull from whenever a negative thought arises.

Tips for Self-Compassion

I tell my clients all the time: *This work is so hard*. It's rewarding, of course, especially as you begin to see changes and improvements, but getting to that place takes a great deal of patience and self-compassion. It can be uncomfortable to look at ourselves so intently and to unearth negative beliefs and thoughts, especially when childhood experiences or previous trauma is a factor.

- Give yourself grace and patience. Say out loud, "I am doing the best I can right now."

- Feel the feelings, whatever they are. Say to yourself, "I am feeling _____ right now, and that is okay."

- Set small goals for yourself. Practice pride.

- Take breaks. It's okay to put aside this work and focus on something else for a while.

STRATEGIES

Use the following strategies to become receptive to identifying and reframing negative thoughts and beliefs.

- Tell someone you trust that you are beginning this work. Ask them to point out when you are being unnecessarily hard on yourself. Those moments are likely to be correlated with the presence of negative self-talk. Use this information as a starting point to begin your awareness of how your negative thoughts influence your confidence.

- Use a personal reward system. When you identify and reframe a negative thought, celebrate, whether it's a relaxing bubble bath, a new journal, or a piece of chocolate. Come up with your own rules for the rewards. One rule could be: At the end of the week, if I have consistently reframed at least one negative thought per day into a more helpful statement, I can treat myself to sushi with friends.

- Recognize that beating yourself up about past events is not helpful. Let go of any mistakes you've made and any reasons or justifications for these negative beliefs. If you notice you're worrying about the past and all the should haves, take a step back and practice your self-care and mindfulness exercises to bring you back to the present.

Putting Strategies into Practice

Let's revisit Sarah and see how she implemented these strategies.

Sarah begins paying very close attention to her inner monologue. Every time she notices she is being especially critical of herself, she reframes the thought to one that is kinder and more helpful. Eventually, she begins to practice a healthier mindset—thinking more positive thoughts, being gentle with herself. When she has a feeling, she validates it. Then she asks herself questions to get to the root of the feeling and the thoughts behind it.

Sarah is shocked to see how her long-held beliefs about herself have influenced her behavior, thoughts, and self-confidence. She begins replacing her negative thoughts with more helpful ones and her overall happiness slowly improves. She is especially surprised to realize how long she has been telling herself that she is responsible for the happiness of others and it is her job to make sure her parents and siblings are okay. She was feeling so resentful, but could not pinpoint why. Once she realizes it is okay to put her needs first, she is able to take care of herself and still check in with her family occasionally.

After beginning the work to change her inner thoughts, Sarah begins to focus on what makes her happy. She begins exercising and getting out of her house more frequently. She adopts a cat to decrease feelings of loneliness since the breakup. She finishes her master's program with a B average and tells herself that is perfectly fine. She keeps her pitcher filled so she has extra to pour into others if and when she chooses.

The next chapter continues Sarah's story and explores how she was able to establish new core beliefs to complement her newly reframed negative thoughts.

CHAPTER 6

Establishing New Core Beliefs

Another useful cognitive tool is establishing new core beliefs. Similar to the cognitive reframing in chapter 5, this strategy focuses not only on the thoughts that are negatively contributing to your daily life, but also on the core beliefs you are reinforcing through inaccurate thinking patterns. Think of the core beliefs as your personal rule book. We will discuss those thinking patterns, known as cognitive distortions, but let's take another look at how Sarah transformed her confidence by using the tools in this book.

In chapter 5, Sarah learned to reframe her negative thoughts to help decrease anxiety and increase self-esteem. In this chapter, she takes this practice a step further and identifies the thinking habits that led to those negative core beliefs that were inhibiting her confidence and happiness.

Sarah, like many women who grow up with the titles of *responsible, mature,* and *good girl,* developed a way of thinking that led her to believe she was either all good or all bad, all the time. When she made mistakes, she saw them as huge disasters and dwelled on them for weeks, which sharply curbed her motivation to try new things or step outside her comfort zone. She had strong reactions to her manager's and colleagues' suggestions and ideas because she believed that in order to be smart and capable, she had to be right all the time. She responded negatively to critique or criticism, believing it overwhelmed all her positive progress. Over time, Sarah became uncomfortable putting herself out there, whether at school, at work, or in social situations.

Negative Core Beliefs

There are numerous cognitive distortions, or inaccurate ways of thinking, that reinforce negative emotions and thoughts. These distortions feel true, but they are actually the result of your brain's effort to make connections, even when connections do not exist or are incorrect. The resulting inaccurate thoughts shore up your bad feelings about yourself and your judgments of others.

Low self-confidence can usually be tied to one (or more) of these inaccurate thinking patterns. These patterns also have the tendency to feed off each other, and it is common to have multiple thought patterns that lead to the same negative core belief.

The most common cognitive distortions are outlined here. You will see Sarah's negative core beliefs reflected in several. How many do you recognize in your own thought patterns?

All-or-Nothing Thinking

Also known as black-and-white thinking, this cognitive distortion is characterized by the belief that all people, things, and events are inherently good or bad, wrong or right, true or false, with no possibility of middle ground or shades of gray. You're either all in or all out. There is no in-between. The trouble with this type of thinking is that mistakes become proof of poor character or incompetence, rather than learning experiences. Another dangerous aspect of this type of thinking is that you look at other people through the same distorted view, which can lead to unfair judgment and lack of tolerance.

When Sarah thinks that making straight As is the only option for future success, she is telling herself that anything less than an A makes her unsuccessful. She has set herself up for decreased confidence if she is unable to get an A. When she makes mistakes and believes this is indicative of her incompetence, this is another example of how all-or-nothing thinking patterns can lead to limiting core beliefs. You can see how this can then spill over into Sarah's personal life and relationships.

Shoulds and Musts

Shoulds and musts are ways of thinking that follow specific rules. Sarah thinks she should be a good daughter and sister, she must visit her family frequently, and she should take care of them. Putting this pressure on herself leads to resentment, as she recognized when she was working to identify the root of her negative thinking patterns. Now she can see which thought processes contributed to the development of these rules.

This cognitive distortion can be tied to all the shoulds and musts women learn as young girls. Some are self-taught, as women often put unreasonable expectations on themselves. No matter their origin, these distorted ways of thinking can lead to decreased self-confidence and self-esteem when it becomes impossible to play by your own rule book.

Jumping to Conclusions

When we jump to conclusions, we make assumptions about someone else's motivations, future actions, or thoughts. When Sarah's friend Ann canceled plans at the last minute because she wasn't feeling well, Sarah immediately assumed Ann no longer wanted to be friends, but it is far more likely that Ann canceled because she had a headache. Her action has nothing to do with Sarah, but Sarah's inaccurate thoughts lead her to that conclusion. This thought that results from the cognitive distortion can become a negative core belief: *I am not likable. People do not want to be my friend.*

Personalization

Not everything is about you. Most people are making decisions based on what is best for themselves, their families, and their work. Allowing your thoughts to make this personal does not serve you and only increases unhappiness.

When Sarah receives corrective criticism from her manager about a work project, she thinks, *I knew he didn't like me. He's so critical of everything I do.* She is using personalization. Rather than assuming her manager cares about the outcome and wants her to succeed, she is allowing distorted thinking to make a connection that does not exist. Her manager's feelings toward her may have nothing to do with his critique, but her thinking process causes her to make this erroneous connection. This leads to a negative viewpoint of not only herself but also her manager, and her experience in the workplace suffers as a result.

Negative Predictions

Also known as catastrophizing, this type of thinking leads to focusing on one negative aspect and maximizing it to great importance. Sarah's tendency toward all-or-nothing thinking goes well with this cognitive distortion because she frequently turns one negative—usually a critique or a mistake—into a prediction of future failure.

Sarah went on a blind date with a woman who never called her afterward. Sarah catastrophized this event, thinking, *I will never find my soulmate.* She allowed her thoughts to maximize one incident to gigantic proportions and make an erroneous prediction about the future.

If Sarah was not using this distorted thinking process, she may have thought that although this woman was not a good match, the right person and relationship was out there. This would lead to more confidence, and Sarah would be more open to future opportunities to meet other people, which would increase the likelihood of this belief becoming reality.

Filtering

Another negative type of thinking occurs when you filter out positive details in favor of negative ones. Sarah's thoughts frequently follow this pattern. She focuses on her perceived failures while completely discounting all the things she does well. This is especially apparent in her assessment of her physical attributes and abilities at work. Sarah focuses on the negatives *(My nose is too big, I need to lose weight)* instead of using positive self-talk *(My eyes are my best physical feature, I have a beautiful smile).* Her thinking patterns literally filter out and disregard the positives.

Overgeneralizing

Using one incident, statement, or moment to make assumptions about yourself or someone else is known as overgeneralizing. When Sarah makes one mistake at work and immediately thinks, *I never do things right*, she is overgeneralizing her abilities in a negative way. Sarah does things right most of the time, but her inaccurate thought process leads her to use this event to make the wrong assumption, which also contributes to negative self-talk and her decreased self-confidence.

She interprets her manager's comments as being overly critical, which turns into a core belief that he is always critical. Overgeneralizing turns into rules about yourself and others, which can become negative core beliefs.

Blaming

Just as you are not responsible for the happiness of others, others are not responsible for your happiness. Blaming is when you hold others accountable for your feelings, actions, or consequences. If you notice this kind of thinking (*She made me feel so guilty, It's his fault I made this mistake, She made me feel stupid in that meeting*), you are using this thought process. Blaming takes away your power to control your thoughts and emotions, and places it on others. This leads to core beliefs that you are not in control of your emotions or that others have all the power, which decreases your self-confidence.

Reasoning Based on Emotion

Emotions are powerful, but they do not always reflect the truth.

When Sarah feels an overwhelming sense of responsibility for her parents and siblings, does that mean that she is truly responsible for them? Of course not. But because she feels it so acutely, this distortion leads her to believe it is the truth, which then influences her core beliefs and subsequent decisions.

Fantasy of Control

So much of our behavior, thoughts, and actions comes from the idea that control is good and keeps you safe. When you worry about the future, it does not prevent bad things from happening, insulate you from future pain, or prepare you to handle the worst. Fantasy of control is the inaccurate belief that we have absolute control over everything. When things do not work out as you intended, your confidence decreases—which is unfortunate, because it was likely not in your control in the first place. If you find yourself becoming extremely frustrated when you are stuck in traffic, pay attention to the negative beliefs swirling in your mind, like *I should have known not to go this way*. This kind of thinking indicates that fantasy of control is distorting your thought process by suggesting you could have predicted or controlled this outcome.

Practice control over your emotions, behavior, and reactions. Recognize when your thoughts are being distorted by the inaccurate idea that you have control over the weather, traffic, or other people's emotions, behaviors, and reactions.

EXERCISE:
Chain of Questions

When faced with a negative thought or fear of a negative outcome, ask yourself "What then?" Follow each response with "What then?" until you get to the root cause or bigger implication of why a negative outcome is frightening you. Identifying the worst-case scenario and recognizing that it is not that scary can help you let go of the fear of a negative outcome. If you look at the worst possible outcome and acknowledge you could handle it, even if it's not ideal, you have taken away the power of the unknown.

Establishing New Core Beliefs

Once you are aware of the cognitive distortions that are driving your thought processes, you can more easily recognize when you are using them to make inaccurate connections. Developing this skill takes time and patience. Much like your automatic negative thoughts, negative core beliefs about yourself and your world can have a tremendous effect on your confidence and self-esteem. These core beliefs take the negative thoughts to a deeper level, where they become ingrained ways of making connections. The core beliefs become your personal rule book in influencing how you live, act, and relate to others.

Establishing new core beliefs is exciting new territory. Visualize this process as throwing out the old maps and establishing your own paths to happiness and confidence.

Understand Past Events

Although you do not want to dwell in the past, evaluating previous events can be helpful in understanding why certain thoughts and beliefs have taken hold. You learned your negative beliefs from other people, as a result of experiences, or as a method of self-preservation or protection from feelings that may have seemed dangerous or overwhelming.

Everyone uses these inaccurate thought processes occasionally because our brains have a negative bias, which means it's easier to focus on negative events and make negative connections when trying to make sense of the world. But with practice, we can make those connections more positive and automatic. One way to practice these positive switches is to focus on the good side of a negative core belief.

Focus on the Good

A useful process in changing negative beliefs is flipping them around to a positive statement, and then looking for evidence that the positive statement is correct. For example, when the negative belief *I'm not good enough for that new position* is flipped into a positive statement, it becomes *I am good enough for that new position.* Focus on the evidence to support this: *I work hard, I always try my best, I am loyal to the company, my customers can depend on me.*

Another common negative belief I hear in my practice is *I'm not a good enough mother.* In session, I flip this into the positive statement *I am a good enough mother,* and then ask the client to provide the evidence that this is true. Eventually she will come up with statements such as *I feed my children, I keep them safe, I take care of them when they are sick, I tell them I love them.* This leads her to discover more and more evidence that the statement is true, which challenges the negative core belief.

Remember Sarah's negative self-statements from chapter 5? Let's take this a step further and identify which cognitive distortions she is using to perpetuate her negative thinking.

NEGATIVE SELF-STATEMENTS	IDENTIFY DISTORTIONS	REBUTTAL
I am fat and ugly.	**FILTERING**	*I have a beautiful smile. My big brown eyes are my best physical feature.*
This project has to be perfect.	**ALL-OR-NOTHING THINKING**	*This project had to get done. It does not have to be perfect.*
I'll never finish in time.	**NEGATIVE PREDICTIONS**	*Just because I am running behind does not mean it will not get done.*
I have to help my family.	**SHOULDS AND MUSTS**	*I can be a good sister and daughter by setting good boundaries and reasonable expectations.*
They need me. I'm the responsible one.	**REASONING BASED ON EMOTION**	*Just because this FEELS like my responsibility does not mean that is the truth.*

Try any of these strategies to keep you in a positive mindset:

- Make a visual reminder of positive beliefs you are working to uphold. Use a combination of uplifting phrases and quotes to keep you in this mindset. Find phrases and quotes online that resonate with you, take screenshots, and keep them in a folder in your phone. Print them out and use them to decorate your walls, write them directly on sticky notes, or use them to start a vision board.

- Try to spend more time with people who are also working on maintaining positivity and confidence in themselves. Confidence is contagious.

- Recognize these cognitive distortions in others around you. Give them grace and patience, as they may not have the same understanding you recently gained, but do limit exposure to their negativity and distorted beliefs.

- As always, practice self-care and compassion. This work takes time, but it is worth it.

Putting Strategies into Practice

Let's see how Sarah's doing.

Sarah realizes her negative core beliefs about herself and others around her have caused so much of her struggles with self-confidence. She recognizes that her tendency to filter out positive thoughts and messages in favor of negative ones has led her to erroneously believe she is not attractive or worthy of love. Her all-or-nothing thinking and negative predictions have held her back from new people and experiences. All the negative message she has internalized became core beliefs or rules about herself.

Once Sarah learned about cognitive distortions, she decided to pay even more attention to her thought processes—not just focusing on the negative thoughts themselves, but also evaluating how she came to those conclusions in the first place. She began flipping around these negative core beliefs and asked herself questions such as, "In what ways am I attractive? In what ways am I likable? How do I show I am good enough at work?" Once she has rebuttals for her most damaging negative core beliefs, she can begin establishing healthier new core beliefs about herself and others.

Sarah continues to reframe negative thoughts as they arise, using the skills she has learned. She has built up an additional strategy to increasing her self-confidence—targeting those deeply held beliefs that negatively impacted her connection with herself and others.

CHAPTER 7

Facing Fears and Moving Forward

Jasmine is a 33-year-old single mother of an 8-year-old son. She and her son recently moved to a new city, leaving behind an emotionally abusive ex-husband in an effort to start over again. The past few years have been incredibly stressful, as she was involved in a drawn-out legal custody battle. She is relieved it is over, although she knows her ex will always be in her life because of their son. All those years of being told she was stupid, crazy, worthless, and not a good mother have left deep scars in her self-esteem. Jasmine was previously a bubbly, energetic, happy woman, but the years of emotional and mental abuse have turned her into someone she does not recognize.

Jasmine is a labor and delivery nurse, and just began a new job at a major hospital. She is passionate about what she does, and loves helping women bring babies into the world. At work, Jasmine feels confident. She knows she is a good nurse, and she knows how to advocate for her patients and keep them safe. She focuses on her patients and her charting, and that's all. She is pleasant in her interactions with her co-workers, but generally keeps to herself. Years of being isolated from other women because of her ex-husband's controlling personality and abuse have led her to feel awkward in social situations. It has been so many years since Jasmine had a female friend that the idea of getting to know someone is extremely daunting.

Jasmine's son will be starting third grade at a new school. He is very excited, and has already befriended other boys in the neighborhood who will be attending the same school. Jasmine is petrified at the idea of meeting the other mothers. She knows she appears aloof and standoffish, but she desperately wants and needs friends to support her through single motherhood. When she thinks about reaching out, however, her chest becomes tight. She tells herself she is being ridiculous, that it should not be so scary to make friends. But she is still afraid. When she finds herself in social situations with new people, she has an overwhelming sense of fear and agitation, like she is coming out of her own skin. She feels incredibly exposed and self-conscious. All she can focus on is the desire to escape.

This chapter explains how Jasmine uses tools from exposure therapy to help her slowly increase her confidence and decrease her fear response.

Using Exposure Therapy to Overcome Fears

Fear is a powerful deterrent. It is actually a survival mechanism, a chemical reaction in the lizard part of the brain that is designed to recognize danger and survive. The fight-or-flight response is necessary for the survival of any species, but when that response is activated inappropriately, it can feel impossible to get yourself out of the danger mindset. People who experience anxiety know that everything in their brains screams "DANGER, DANGER, DANGER!" even if the situation is not, in fact, dangerous. Their bodies react physically with an elevation in heart and respiratory rates, tightness in the chest, maybe even a wave of heat, numbness, or tingling. Their fight-or-flight response is so elevated and overactive, it lies about the true nature of the situation or event. With simple phobias, post-traumatic stress disorder, and other anxiety disorders, the brain makes an incorrect connection between danger and an event, an object, or a situation. The elevated response may continue even when the immediate danger ends, such as in incidents of abuse, trauma, or peril. The primary goal of exposure therapy is retraining the brain to learn there is no danger. This is commonly used to treat anxiety disorders.

Exposure therapy works by purposefully exposing you to an event, an object, or a scenario, real or imagined, that evokes high levels of distress and panic. The exposure is conducted in a controlled environment with a trained therapist present to provide support and teach relaxation and coping skills along the way. Over the course of the exposure, you learn that you are safe, that there is no need to escape or use compulsive behaviors to decrease anxiety because you have been desensitized to the feared situation or object.

Exposure therapy can be divided into three categories. *In vivo exposure* is done in real life. For example, in treatment for phobia of spiders, a client would be exposed to the source of anxiety (a spider) in person. Imagined exposure uses the client's thoughts and memories of a real or perceived threat as the exposure. In a case of a military veteran with post-traumatic stress disorder, vivid memories of the traumatizing events would be used, rather than placing the person in a real-life traumatic scenario. *Interoceptive exposure therapy* uses purposeful exposure to bodily sensations of panic and anxiety, such as elevated heart rate and shortness of breath, to desensitize the client to the fear response.

You can use exposure therapy to help you overcome fears, and it will inevitably lead to increased confidence.

Exposure Therapy Step by Step

Here are specific steps for using exposure therapy to confront and overcome fears. Start with the least amount of anxiety or fear and slowly build up layers of confidence. This is also known as a fear hierarchy, or a list of specific scenarios and situations that cause you fear and anxiety. The list is typically ordered from the least scary task to the most feared. You may spend more time at one step than another. For each task you accomplish, your confidence will grow, but stay at each level until you feel confident in moving forward.

Here is Jasmine's fear hierarchy:

1. At her son's new school, ask another mom where to find a particular classroom or office.

2. Give a fellow mom a compliment.

3. Sign up to volunteer at the school on days she is not scheduled to work.

4. Introduce herself to another mom.

5. Invite one of the neighborhood boys over to play with her son.

6. Invite a mom to coffee after drop-off one morning.

Notice how Jasmine's list increases in intensity. She begins with asking another mom a simple question that does not require a long conversation. Complimenting someone can be done in passing and does not require more than one sentence. The list ends with Jasmine inviting another mom to coffee, an idea that causes her to experience intense fear and anxiety. Her fear response is too elevated to do this immediately, but as she begins with something less scary and proves to herself that nothing bad happens, her confidence slowly builds up.

Tips for Successful Exposure Therapy

The most important aspect of using these strategies is making sure your fear hierarchy is appropriate. Remember to start with tasks that cause only minimal anxiety, and increase slightly with each step. Keep the steps small to avoid feeling overwhelmed and experiencing excess fear. Similar to accomplishing small goals, as discussed in chapter 2, your confidence will increase with each step. It is okay if you repeat some steps. For example, Jasmine may compliment several moms before she feels comfortable signing up to volunteer in the classroom.

Practice relaxation and meditation exercises before and after you tackle each step. Visualize yourself successfully completing the task. Repeat mantras to keep yourself full of positive thoughts, such as *Nothing bad is happening, My anxiety is lying to me, I can do this, There's nothing to be afraid of.*

JOURNAL EXERCISE:
Develop Your Own Fear Hierarchy

Using Jasmine's fear hierarchy as an example, write out your own fear hierarchy in a step-by-step format. Remember to start small and expose yourself gradually to an increasing level of discomfort before eventually building up to the main fear. This can be a fear of public speaking, a fear of elevators, a fear of social events—anything.

Overcoming Fear of Failure

Fear is a biological and chemical response to real or imagined danger. It is a protective instinct designed for self-preservation. Your body responds to an emotional threat the same way that it responds to a physical one. The problem is when the intensity of the response does not line up with the actual danger.

If you have made an inaccurate connection between failure and danger, you likely have a deeply held core belief that failure is not an option. *Failure is dangerous. To fail is to let my family down. To fail is to let myself down.* This core belief may be the cause of the anxiety you feel when you think of failing or making a mistake. If this resonates with you, run this core belief through the strategies you learned in chapter 6. Find the evidence to refute this belief. Redefine what it means to fail. Is it really failure if you tried your best but the outcome was not what you expected or wanted? Or does the true definition of failure have more to do with not trying in the first place? Only you can answer that, but I encourage you to work toward acceptance of the latter definition.

It is okay to worry about an outcome. It is okay to want to get it right. But if you think mistakes make you any less of the amazing person you are, check that belief at the door because it is no longer welcomed in your new confident thinking patterns.

Remember, it's most important that you give yourself the opportunity to make these changes. Once you've made the decision to overcome these fears, you owe it to yourself to try. No one can do this work for you, but no one has as much to gain as you do.

Use the following tips to help you maintain confidence and overcome any fears about the outcome of this process.

Acknowledge Your Feelings

Remember the self-compassion tips from chapter 5? One is worth repeating: Acknowledge and validate your feelings. *I am feeling [overwhelmed, scared, unsure, nervous] right now, and that's okay. I see you. I hear you. I feel you. But I am not going to let this stop me.*

Feelings don't go away when we ignore them. They build and build until they explode all over the people around us, and the fallout is not appealing. Telling yourself that your feelings are silly or unreasonable is not helpful; it only diminishes your confidence because you are saying your feelings don't matter. Although our feelings are not necessarily always helpful or accurate, they are still worth acknowledging. Distract yourself from the negative feeling, put it in a box up on a shelf, and refocus on getting through your fear hierarchy, one step at a time. If you can identify the thoughts that are leading to the negative feelings, run them through a thought record and reframe them. Get to the root of the feelings, but never discount or dismiss them. Your feelings will grow stronger if you do not acknowledge them.

Keep Your Sense of Humor

This work can grow tiring, and you may become discouraged. Be sure to find joy and humor in the process. Don't take yourself too seriously. If you mess up, embarrass yourself, or have a setback, it's okay. Sometimes laughter really is the best medicine, and keeping your sense of humor will help you remain positive and on track. Not to mention you'll be more fun to be around.

Change Your Stress Mindset

Some research suggests that people who see stress in a positive way—as a challenge, for example—tend to be happier and more motivated than those who see stress as debilitating or capable of ruining their day or their health. Those who view stress positively also perform better on cognitive tasks. This is important, because if you are able to reframe any automatic thoughts about stress into something more positive, you can change your stress mindset. If you overslept, spilled coffee on your shirt, and got a flat tire on the way to an important work event, modify your thoughts to view the stress in a more positive way. Rather than, *Can this @#$* day get any worse?*, reframe the situation using a healthier mindset: *What a challenging day. Bring it on, I can handle it!*

Choosing to embody a positive stress mindset keeps you in line with the other strategies you have learned and contributes to building confidence. As you go through stressful events, remind yourself that each one is an opportunity to learn, to increase your resilience, and to prove you are capable and strong. You will become more and more confident as you realize you got through it, even if you had to claw or crawl along the way.

Find People Who Can Support You

Having positive, supportive friends and family members who are behind you 100 percent can make a huge difference, especially if you need a little extra motivation. Overcoming fears takes commitment—not just in terms of time, but also mental and emotional work. Make sure those around you support your efforts and don't let you feel guilty about taking care of yourself. If they understand what you're doing, they'll be less likely to complain if you're a bit distracted, and more likely to encourage you during setbacks.

If your friends and family aren't behind you, find support elsewhere. Join a local community or church group that is in line with your goals. Find an online community. Schedule an appointment with a local counselor or life coach. We are creatures of connection, and you need people in your corner who are rooting for you.

Continuing Your Practice

This book has covered a tremendous amount of information. Some you may have learned through previous therapy experiences or from self-help books. Some may have been described in a different way. I hope you're able to recognize the infinite possibilities open to you as a result of knowing this information, whether it's your first time learning it or your tenth. Read through this book a second time if you can. Another read often gives you additional insight and a different level of awareness. Something new may click, or another connection or idea may come to mind.

Please also visit the Resources (page 115) as well as the list of recommended books (page 117) I have found particularly helpful for my clients.

Practice

Practice makes perfect, right? When you are working on making major changes in your thinking patterns and overall belief system, practice and repetition keep these new positive connections solid, so even when you have setbacks you can return to more helpful ways of thinking.

Continue practicing the tips and strategies you've learned in this book. Occasionally revisit thought records and reread your journal. Continue setting small, achievable goals for yourself every month. Practice gratitude daily. Practice mindfulness and relaxation strategies. Take care of yourself physically and emotionally.

Make Long-Term Goals

Setting small short-term goals is useful for keeping you motivated and engaged, especially in the early days of building self-confidence. As you continue on this journey, you may want to expand on the goals you developed for yourself in chapter 2, and I encourage you to do so.

Once you have improved your self-confidence, there's really no limit to where you can take it. Where do you see yourself one year from now? Five years from now? Are you married with two children and a dog, driving a minivan and living in the suburbs? Are you CEO of a major publishing company, with hundreds of employees and your own personal assistant? Are you healthy, happy, and content? Are you changing the world, traveling the world, exploring the world? Who do you want to be with? Take some time to think about your long-term goals so you stay focused on your growth and forward progress.

Plan for Setbacks

Setbacks will happen. If you've ever attempted to sleep train an infant, start an exercise routine, or support someone through an addiction, you know they are inevitable. You may have relapses, and that's okay. Here are some common setbacks along the road to increased self-confidence:

Finding yourself back in negative thinking patterns. Practice forgiveness and know this is part of the process. As soon as you notice the negative thoughts returning, practice the strategies you learned in chapter 5. Use a thought record to reframe negative thoughts, recite your mantras, and practice self-compassion.

Getting out of newly acquired healthy sleep, eating, or exercise habits. Recognize you've made the slip, give yourself grace, and adjust. You've established these healthy habits before, and you can do it again.

Becoming drawn into other people's drama and negativity. If you find yourself becoming unnecessarily drawn into someone else's negativity, take a step back and re-evaluate the relationship. Is this your circus and your monkeys? If so, what steps can you take to bring about peace and positivity? If it's not your business, how do you detach with love from the drama and maintain some separation moving forward?

Don't Forget Self-Care!

In case you haven't figured it out, I am a huge advocate for women taking excellent care of themselves spiritually, emotionally, mentally, socially, financially, professionally, and physically. Make your own list of self-care categories, and come up with at least three activities or practices you can complete in different amounts of time.

For example, Jasmine's self-care strategies would look like this:

	5–10 MIN	15–30 MIN	30+ MIN
SPIRITUAL	Say a prayer	Read bible passages	Attend a church service or bible study
EMOTIONAL	Make a gratitude list for the day	Sit outside in the sunshine	Have a movie night with son
PHYSICAL	Do yoga or stretch	Cook a healthy meal	Exercise
SOCIAL	Text a friend	Call a friend or family member	Meet a friend for lunch
MENTAL	Meditate / Work a crossword puzzle	Read a good book in a bubble bath	Take a mental health day off work

Once you are clear on some concrete ways to increase your self-care practice, do at least one in each category per week. Filling yourself up is an excellent way to maintain and celebrate your progress, plus you will have more energy and desire to spend quality time with the people you love.

Have Patience with Yourself

Be patient with yourself in every phase of this process. I know it can be difficult when you seem to be progressing at a snail's pace, but remember this is a marathon, not a sprint. You are making significant changes in your thinking patterns, core beliefs, and fear responses. This is not small stuff, and it definitely does not happen overnight. Real change takes practice and time to develop new ways of thinking and believing. If you become frustrated, go back to the mantras (*I am doing the best I can right now, and that's okay*), acknowledge the feelings (*I am feeling frustrated right now, and that's okay*), and recognize how far you've come. Small steps are not insignificant. Every achievement, big and small, is moving you closer to your main goal.

Celebrate Every Step

Practice gratitude in every step you take. Be thankful for the journey. You are an amazing creature, and you were put in this world for a reason. You have the capacity to work toward these changes, no matter how long it takes. For every obstacle you overcome, for every moment that brings you pride, practice gratitude. Celebrate every moment of progress. Each step is necessary, each learning experience brings new knowledge, and even the tiniest bit of progress is getting you to your goal of enjoying more self-confidence.

Tips for overcoming setbacks:

> **View setbacks as learning opportunities.** What can you learn from a setback? What do you know now that you didn't before? How can you use this to guide you through your journey?

> **Keep up with your journaling practice.** Record successes and setbacks and view them as reinforcement in your ability to succeed and overcome setbacks because you have done it before.

> **Remember to practice self-care.** How are you caring for yourself right now, physically and emotionally? Are you pushing too hard? Are you taking breaks? Are you doing too much for others? Be very mindful of your need for rest, exercise, and boundaries.

Strategies for maintaining a growth mindset:

> **Journal about your end goals.** Be very clear about your long-term vision for yourself. Assume you have all the tools and confidence you need to achieve anything you desire,

and write it down. Add it to a vision board and make it part of your daily gratitude practice.

Be prepared for relationships to change. You may lose touch with friends whose worldviews are not in line with your newly acquired positivity. You may gain new friends who help you be a better version of yourself. Don't apologize. You deserve to surround yourself with people who help you continue your path to confidence. Your family members may be upset or confused about your newfound confidence and boundaries. Encourage them to join you on this journey, but recognize you cannot take responsibility for their happiness.

Visualize yourself becoming more confident about something you previously feared. Use this visualization in a relaxation method. When practicing meditation exercises, focus on the word "confidence."

Practice self-compassion. Do one of the exercises from chapter 5 every day.

Putting Strategies into Practice

Let's revisit Jasmine and see how she implemented these strategies.

Jasmine is determined to decrease her social anxiety, not just for herself but also for her son. She knows her previous marriage damaged her self-confidence, but she also recognizes that she is a strong, capable woman. On her way to drop off her son on his first day of school, she uses silent positive mantras to encourage herself. She listens to her son's excited chatter and is reminded of her motivation.

While walking her son into school, Jasmine approaches a mom she recognizes from the neighborhood and asks for directions to the third-grade classrooms. Her heart is pounding, but she reminds herself that nothing bad is happening. The woman is very friendly, and walks Jasmine straight to the classroom. While returning to her car, Jasmine congratulates herself for taking that first step. Now that she has completed one level of her fear hierarchy, she realizes she feels slightly more confident about herself and thinks, "Maybe I really can do this."

Over the course of the next few weeks, Jasmine slowly moves up the fear hierarchy, sometimes repeating her steps, but with different women. Everything goes well until she comes to the final step. She experiences a setback. She opens her mouth to invite one of the moms to coffee, but freezes. A wave of heat overcomes her, and she asks a question about the upcoming spelling test instead. When Jasmine returns home, she feels very discouraged.

But rather than stew in disappointment and self-loathing, Jasmine decides to be gentle with herself. She returns to her self-care chart, and spends the day doing things that make her feel good about herself. She reminds herself that she has already come so far, and this is her final step. She gains self-confidence through the very act of giving herself that grace, recognizing she has the power to forgive herself, learn from the disappointment, and use it to push forward.

When she returns to school to pick up her son, she runs into the other mom. Before she can lose her nerve, she invites the woman to coffee on her next day off. When her invitation is accepted with a smile, Jasmine feels something inside herself burst open—joy and excitement that overrules the anxiety and fear. She realizes that nothing bad happened, and she feels wonderful and proud of herself.

Just like Jasmine, you can increase your confidence by facing your fears and taking steps to overcome them. Using the strategies throughout this book, you can change your mindset, transform your negative core beliefs, and improve your physical health and relationships. Remember the tips and the suggestions, especially those regarding self-care.

You will find my contact information in the back of the book. I welcome any and all feedback and would love to hear from you. Above all else, know this: you are capable of tremendous strength and courage, and everything you need to be successful at increasing your confidence is already inside of you.

Resources

Helpful books and websites organized by subject category:

Acceptance and Commitment Therapy

ACT Made Simple: *An Easy-To-Read Primer on Acceptance and Commitment Therapy,* by Russ Harris

Addiction

Alcoholics Anonymous www.aa.org

Narcotics Anonymous www.na.org

National Institute on Alcohol Abuse and Alcoholism www.niaaa.nih.gov

Substance Abuse and Mental Health Services Administration www.samhsa.gov or 800-662-4357

The SAMHSA is a confidential and free information service for individuals and family members facing mental and/or substance use disorders. This service provides referrals to local treatment facilities, support groups, and community-based organizations.

Choosing a therapist

Psychology Today offers a search tool that allows you to filter lists of therapists and counselors by gender, specialization, therapeutic approach, zip code, and insurance participation.

www.psychologytoday.com

Codependency

www.al-anon.org

Codependent No More: *How to Stop Controlling Others and Start Caring for Yourself,* by Melody Beattie

Codependent No More Workbook, by Melody Beattie

Beyond Codependency: *And Getting Better All the Time,* by Melody Beattie

Cognitive Behavioral Therapy

The Anxiety and Worry Workbook: *The Cognitive and Behavioral Solution,* by David A. Clark and Aaron T. Beck

Feeling Good: *The New Mood Therapy,* by David D. Burns

Domestic Violence

National Coalition Against Domestic Violence www.ncadv.org

National Domestic Violence Hotline 800-799-7233

Perinatal/Postpartum Support

This Isn't What I Expected: *Overcoming Postpartum Depression,* by Karen R. Kleiman

Good Moms Have Scary Thoughts: *A Healing Guide to the Secret Fears of New Mothers,* by Karen R. Kleiman

Postpartum Support International www.postpartum.net

Relaxation and Meditation Apps

Calm

Expectful (for pregnancy and postpartum)

Headspace

Motivation

Smiling Mind

Self-Help Books

Atomic Habits: *An Easy & Proven Way to Build Good Habits and Break Bad Ones,* by James Clear

Attached: *The New Science of Adult Attachment and How It Can Help You Find—and Keep—Love,* by Amir Levine and Rachel Heller

The Body Keeps the Score: *Brain, Mind, and Body in the Healing of Trauma,* by Bessel van der Kolk

Dare to Lead: *Brave Work. Tough Conversations. Whole Hearts.,* by Brené Brown

Daring Greatly: *How the Courage to Be Vulnerable Transforms the Way We Live, Love, Parent, and Lead,* by Brené Brown

Depression Fallout: *The Impact of Depression on Couples and What You Can Do to Preserve the Bond,* by Anne Sheffield

The Gifts of Imperfection: *Let Go of Who You Think You're Supposed to Be and Embrace Who You Are,* by Brené Brown

You Are a Badass: *How to Stop Doubting Your Greatness and Start Living an Awesome Life,* by Jen Sincero

Sexual Abuse

National Sexual Violence Resource Center www.nsvrc.org

Nonprofit organization providing information and location-specific resources to prevent and respond to sexual violence.

Suicide

National Suicide Prevention Lifeline www.suicidepreven tionlifeline.org or 800-273-8255

References

Ben-Avi, N., S. Toker, and D. Heller. (2018). 'If stress is good for me, it's probably good for you too': Stress mindset and judgment of others' strain. *Journal of Experimental Social Psychology,* 74, 98–110. https://doi.org/10.1016/j.jesp.2017.09.002.

Brown, Brené. (2012). *Daring Greatly: How the Courage to Be Vulnerable Transforms the Way We Live, Love, Parent, and Lead,* Penguin Random House, New York, NY.

Crum, A. J., M. Akinola, A. Martin, S. Fath. (2017). The role of stress mindset in shaping cognitive, emotional, and physiological responses to challenging and threatening stress. *Anxiety, Stress & Coping*, 30(4):379–395. https://doi.org/10.1080/10615806.2016.1275585.

Cuddy, Amy. (2015). *Presence: Bringing Your Boldest Self to Your Biggest Challenges,* Little, Brown and Company, New York, NY.

Dweck, Carol S. (2006). *Mindset: The New Psychology of Success,* Random House, New York, NY.

Novak, B. J. (2014). *The Book with No Pictures.* Penguin Random House, New York, NY.

Sincero, Jen. (2013). *You Are a Badass: How to Stop Doubting Your Greatness and Start Living an Awesome Life,* Running Press, Philadelphia, PA.

Vaish, A., T. Grossmann, and A. Woodward. (2008). Not all emotions are created equal: The negativity bias in social-emotional development. *Psychological Bulletin, 134*(3), 383–403. https://doi.org/10.1037/0033-2909.134.3.383.

Index

Acknowledgments

I would like to sincerely express my wholehearted appreciation for my clients, past and present, who have taught me just how strong, resilient, and courageous women can be. It is a privilege and such a blessing to be a part of your journey.

Thank you to my wonderful husband and children, who were so supportive, encouraging, and patient with me throughout this process. And a huge thank you to everyone at Callisto Media who was involved in this project. I absolutely loved every second of this amazing experience, and I am so grateful for the opportunity to share this information with other women.

About the Author

Leslie Theriot Herhold, MSW, LCSW, PMH-C, has a clinical practice in Lafayette, Louisiana, where she specializes in mental health services for women and provides continuing education workshops on maternal mental health for clinicians and health care providers. She lives in south Louisiana with her husband, two children, and their sweet, goofy Goldendoodle.

Follow her on Facebook and Instagram @leslietherholdlcsw, email her at ltherholdlcsw@outlook.com, and sign up for updates at LeslieTHerholdlCSW.com.

CPSIA information can be obtained
at www.ICGtesting.com
Printed in the USA
JSHW041353100720
6558JS00004B/6

9 781647 391461